AN INTELLIGENT LIFE

AN INTELLIGENT LIFE

BUDDHIST PSYCHOLOGY
OF SELF-TRANSFORMATION

Koitsu Yokoyama

TRANSLATED BY
Varghese Puthuparampil

Wisdom Publications
199 Elm Street
Somerville, MA 02144 USA
wisdompubs.org

Library of Congress Cataloging-in-Publication Data
Yokoyama, Koitsu, 1940–
[Yuishiki to iu ikikata. English]
   An intelligent life : Buddhist psychology of self-transformation / Yokoyama Koitsu.
      pages cm
   Includes index.
   ISBN 1-61429-196-9 (pbk. : alk. paper)
   1. Yogacara (Buddhism) 2. Vijñaptimatrata. I. Yokoyama, Koitsu, 1940– Yuishiki to iu ikikata. Translation of: II. Title.
   BQ7494.Y64513 2015
   294.3'42042—dc23

                         2015000047

ISBN 978-1-61429-196-1
ebook ISBN 978-1-61429-213-5

19 18 17 16 15
6   5   4   3   2

Cover design by Katrina Noble.
Interior design by Gopa&Ted2. Set in Scala Pro 11/17.7.

3 4633 00289 9670

MIX
Paper from
responsible sources
FSC® C011935

Please visit fscus.org.

CONTENTS

I. What Is This Life?

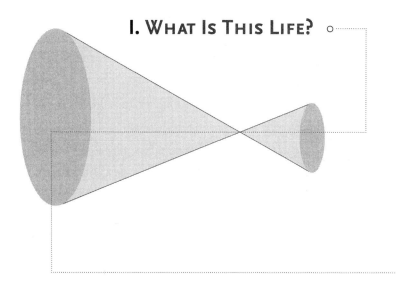

1

THE SEARCH FOR IDENTITY

WHENEVER WE ASK about something, we make use of inter-rogative pronouns. *When* and *where* shall we meet? *What* is this good for? *Why* is it like that? *What* is that? *How* shall we do it? Among all these interrogative pronouns, the most fundamental is "what." For unless the "what" is answered, it is impossible to arrive at a conclusion about the "how." Only after first ascertaining *what* we are can we decide *how* to live. To live without knowledge of *what* we are, is to live like a phantom. It is certainly a mistake.

Little children who are learning how to speak begin asking about things using *what.* On the train it is a very common scene to witness small children pestering their mothers, asking, "Mama, what is that, what is it?" Since children are pure at heart, they never stop asking "what?" But adults, with decades of dis-criminatory thinking behind them, assume that they understand things obviously; they forget to keep asking, "what?" Instead we worry about *how* to live, *how* to do what is best, and so on. Usually we lead a life in accordance with our own desires and craving—a way of life that engenders suffering and worry both to ourselves and to others—but we fail to ever ask: "*What* am I?"

The very first object of the question "what?" should be our self. It will naturally expand to other objects: "What is the other?" "What is nature?" "What is the universe?" This is because oneself exists by the grace of others, oneself lives in nature, and oneself is an individual existence in the universe. It is quite natural to think about the day's schedule in the morning; but would we not do well if, from time to time, we also asked ourselves these philosophical questions? "What is this thing called 'self'?" "Why is this universe like this?"

To be born in this world is a wonderful thing. To be born as a human being, somewhere in the ceaseless flow of time and the unlimited expanse of space, is an expression of the impossible made possible. Don't you strongly feel, deep down, that the miracle of the self's existence—right here and now—is more marvelous than the appearance of a mysterious UFO from somewhere else?

It is a matter of great wonder that the eye has the power of vision. When the eye, a product of atoms and molecules, enters into a cognitive relationship with things, which are themselves made up of atoms and molecules, there arises a conscious vision that perceives nature—mountains, rivers, the sky studded with twinkling stars. In other words, to say "the eye has the power of sight" is nothing short of a miracle. Shall we not go even further and return to the source of the question? Shouldn't we also inquire earnestly about ourselves, about the being that contains this wonderful eye and power of sight and that cognizes this universe?

The world is like a stormy sea in which we are buffeted by the innumerable sufferings of life. It is said that life is a series of four types of suffering—namely, birth, old age, sickness, and death. There are few who are not overwhelmed by these difficulties. But if we can keep up a spirit of inquiry—a spirit that always asks, "What is this?"—then we will not falter in the face of adversity.

Before ever asking, "How should I live?" let's start by asking, with a childlike spirit, "What is this life?" Let's even cry out from the bottom of our heart: "What is this?" This cry will stir awakening by inspiring the altruistic will that lies dormant in the deepest layers of ourselves. Doing so, we will certainly find the courage to say, "Yes, I will live!"

Generally, we think that there is a world outside us, and it is in this outside world that other people, things, nature, and the entire universe exist. But is this thinking really correct? No, it is not, because each one of us creates a world of ourselves, and being enclosed in it, cannot possibly leave it.

The world is understood in two ways: as a *tangible* world of experience and as an *abstract* world. The former is the world that each person creates. We think that we live in a world common to all, but in truth this is not the case. Each one of us is in fact enclosed in a universe of his or her own experiences. For example, if I am not in a pleasant mood, the world has already become dark. If a thorn pricks my finger, the world has already become painful. No other person can directly experience my pleasant or painful feelings.

As long as the ego remains, we cannot get out of the world of our private experiences. Since we have never slipped its confines, how then can we really talk about a world "outside" of ourselves? It could be that "outside" is nothing more than just a word. But even if there is an outside world and people come to a consensus about its existence, it still remains an abstract world for us.

Everything I experience exists in my own mind. For instance, let's take the example of money, which is an object of great attachment for all. Whenever I see money I automatically presume two things: that money exists apart from me, and that it exists externally, exactly as I see it. Is this thinking right? No. It's nothing more than my own strong mental image. Granted, there may indeed be something out there to which I respond; but as already indicated, I am shut up within a world of experience that I create, and it is impossible for me to get outside of it. Therefore, I cannot directly see or touch whatever is truly external to me.

Thus we can conclude that the money that I see now is only an image in my mind. If my state of mind changes, the image also changes. For instance, if I am drunk, my vision of money becomes blurred. Other people may object that this is only because I am drunk, and consequently my brain is not functioning normally. They will insist that the money really does perfectly exist, irrespective of my blurred image of it.

But we must ask in return: can we really consider the world that is created by a "normal" brain (one that is free from intoxication, for example) to be a "normal" real world? It is true that we can safely say that the world seen with unintoxicated eyes and an unintoxicated brain is a "normal" world. However, it is only "normal" insofar as we recognize it and arrive at a consensus among ourselves by collectively speaking about it as "normal." We distinguish between "normal" and "abnormal," but since we do not know anything other than these two categories, it is impossible for us to judge what is ultimately normal and what is ultimately abnormal.

The money that I see is certainly a phantom of my mind. This is just one possible example; it is not a question of just money alone. What about the self that I recognize as myself, and you,

FIGURE 1: A SINGLE PERSON, A SINGLE WORLD

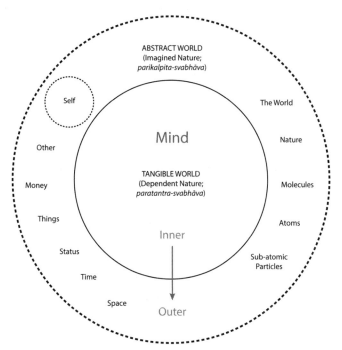

Imagined Nature: the abstract world spoken in language; object of attachment.

Dependent Nature: Mind; things that arise due to causes and conditions.

"the other" to my self, and nature, which envelops both self and other, and the universe, which comprises everything—do all these really exist outside of me? Or are the universe, nature, self, and other—all of which I tangibly experience—only shadows in my mind as was the case with money? In fact, we might say of ourselves that we are "a single person, a single world," for we are entirely unable to get beyond the confinement of ourselves.

Why can we not escape from the captivity of ourselves? The answer is very simple: it is because our experiences are characterized by what we may call an "ego consciousness." As long as we are possessed by this "ego consciousness"—which we ordinarily refer to as "I," "myself," or "me"—we will be incapable of evading our own mind. So all of our activities end up always centered on the self, on "egoism." A charitable act done for another, in the final analysis, remains an act done for oneself.

Consider the concept of loving others. Can we really love others in a selfless and disinterested way? In fact, when we love others, our ego consciousness expects them to return our love. The other is expected to give way, lest I run into him on the road. As the train comes to the platform, and the door opens, I run to get a seat first. Everywhere, the ego consciousness is subtly performing its work. Is it really good to live life through such actions?

Does this "self," "I," or "me" actually exist? We conceive that we ourselves do exist, and our thoughts and actions are concentrated on that existing "me." Still, does such a self in fact exist? No! The self is only an echo of the word *self.* In my career as a professor, I often used the following script to help students grasp this truth.

"Consider your hand." Students look at their hands.

"Whose hand is it?" I ask.

"It's my hand," everyone answers.

"You can see your hand with your own eyes and confirm its objective existence. Can you also turn your thought inward and confirm something within you that corresponds to the word *my*?"

Now the students begin to think deeply. Answers are typically slow to come and hesitantly stated. Many are perplexed. Although we expect words to reveal the existence of what they denote, in the case of *my* or *self* we find nothing that precisely corresponds to these words.

I pose still more questions.

"Please close your eyes." I allow a few moments to pass. "Now open them to see. You certainly see me, because I am standing in front of you. But who is it that sees me?"

Students are typically quick to answer, "*I* am the one who sees you!"

But again, as was the case with the owner of the hand, I ask them to pursue this *I*: "What is it that corresponds precisely to this word *I*?"

Again, they have trouble identifying anything.

In the simple process of questioning our assumed experience, we quickly become aware of the fact that what we take to be ourselves is merely an echo of the word *me*. We are made up of hands, legs, a body, eyeballs, functioning eyesight, and so on and so forth, but this is all. When we attach the word *me* (which has no prior existence of its own) to all these realities, we allow ourselves to fall into thinking that this is *my* hand, *my* foot, that *I* see things, and so on. When we look into this "I," so central to our experiences, we can't figure out where or what it is. Isn't this a high-handed maneuver that contradicts reality?

Let's consider further examples. For instance, seeing a pyramid, I am quick to say, "There is a pyramid." But in truth there are only the stones that have gone into the construction of the pyramid. If we analyze and pick apart these stones themselves, we get only stone powder, molecules, atoms, and finally atomic particles. By taking into account the data of our perception, and concretizing them with words, we create a thing called "pyramid," and subsequently we perceive it to be a real, objective thing.

In the same vein, on reflection we find only mind and body as elements for the constitution of a self. Ultimately the body, like the stones of a pyramid, is an assembly of an infinite number of minute elements. Mind is also comprised of many different moments of mind. A single second of mind is just one part of a complex phenomenon. When the concept of *me* emerges within our experience, we presume that there exists a substance called "me." This is similar to contemporary quantum physics where the smallest units of things are particles like electrons, which do not exist as substances with spatial extension. At the macro level, in the everyday world, we can see that there is a difference between self and other, but that difference is only an illusion—

the result of a pervasive prejudice. If we look more closely at things, digging into what they really are at the micro level, all substantial differences disappear.

So when it comes to the mind, is there really a mind that I can say is "my mind"? Mind has no color or form. Mind is instantaneous, passing from moment to moment like the flame of a candle or the flowing water of a river. The constituent elements of both things and the mind are only the continuous flux and flow of all things. Can we really assert that they are our minds and bodies? Can we really intercept the flux of mind and matter as if they were static? There is only a body and mind where I see "me." The "me" indicated by the thought "This is *my* body and *my* mind" doesn't really exist. When we come to understand this truth, our experience of the world and vision of life is greatly transformed.

Are you outside? Or near a window with a view? Take in the landscape—lush green mountains, the vast, dark-blue expanse of the sky above, whatever you may see—all the beauty of nature unfolds before your eyes. Really, that the eyes can even see at all is such a wonder! We must be grateful for the gift of sight. The Japanese term for "wonderful," *fushigi*, is originally a Buddhist term, derived from the Sanskrit word *acintya* ("unthinkable"), which was then translated in Chinese as "a matter beyond our thinking and speaking."

Why do color and form appear whenever we open our eyes? When the eyes, which are just atoms and particles, make contact with the beauty of nature, which is also constituted of atoms and particles, why is it that in our eye and our mind there arises a consciousness of seeing lush greenery? Mind arises when the world and our organs of sense meet each other. Even though the details may be beyond our understanding, it is a fact that the mind is active here, specifically in what we refer to as vision. We may not understand the *why* or *how* of the reality of the senses, but we can certainly admit that they are wonderful. It isn't just our senses that are wonderful either. Living beings endowed with bodies and minds—even that we are alive as human beings—are a wonder.

Once, as I was leading a seminar at the university where I teach, the students and I discussed why life is important. "Why is life important?" I asked. There came the answer, "Because life is very rare." The birth of life on the face of the earth, in this vast and boundless universe, is indeed a very rare event. Over time, satellites in space have lifted the veil from the heavens, showing us the true faces of the planets and the vast expanse of the night sky. As a result we are now almost certain that there is no life in the solar system other than what is here on Earth. Hence the old Buddhist aphorism that "life is rare and is therefore precious" still has great persuasive power. None of the students opposed this idea. That a thing of rarity is precious is not just a personal feeling, but is a commonly shared value among all people.

It is, of course, also possible to think that there is no need to treat a thing carefully simply because it is rare. One student had the opinion that "life came into being when a favorable condition for the birth of life on earth came about accidentally. Therefore, it is not necessary to consider it as precious." There is some reason in this line of thinking, which brings together the concept of "accident" and the concept of "rare." But another student argued: "This is an insufficient reason. It might have originated accidentally, but life remains precious all the same because of its rarity." At this point, however, I had the impression that we were merely arguing about concepts—not about life itself.

Before making a *value judgment* about whether life is precious or not precious, it is necessary to make a *factual judgment*, which requires a determined awareness of the facts of the matter. We can say that there are two types of judgments—factual judgments and value judgments—and we must begin by making a factual judgment. This is a judgment that is not merely based on the intellect. The statement "Eyes see," and more generally the statement "We are alive," are judgments that we savor prior to rational engagement. These are experiences for us to become one with.

To the degree that one can become fully aware of it, strongly relishing the wonderful fact of being alive engenders a new self-awareness. This new awareness of oneself likewise sees the life in other living things as an object of wonder. A heart filled with wonder at life generates in turn a feeling of respect, which is then transformed into gratitude and finally results in our having a benevolent, compassionate heart towards others. When we come to know *what* reality is, we inevitably come to solve the problem of *how* to live—with love for others.

From time to time, let's close and then open our eyes, closely observe the reality that manifests before us, and take time to quietly relish things.

The *Diamond Cutter Sutra*, a classic Buddhist text, says, "Since sentient beings are not sentient beings, they are sentient beings." If we generalize this expression, it would look something like this: "A is non-A; therefore A." From the perspective of formal logic this is a fallacious statement. But if we base our lives on this logic, it is a very practical idea, one that gives us the vital courage to truly live.

In fact this logic speaks to existence as a whole: once we negate "existence" and return to the source, true existence appears. The term *true* may be too cold an expression in this context; it would be better to say that the fullness of existence appears. To explain what I mean, I would like to relate an incident one of my students shared with me during a seminar. On a trip hiking through the mountains with a mountaineering group, one of the seniors slipped from a cliff and fell into a deep ravine. He was lucky to have caught hold of a branch on the way down, so he was stuck hanging in midair. He surely would have met his death if he had fallen all the way down the ravine. The other students pulled him up, and his life was saved without any injury. Shaken, he slowly sat on a stone and was offered a smoke. As he inhaled he said aloud, "What a delicious thing it is!" His life (A) had first been negated (non-A), and then he came back to life (A). While smoking, he experienced an absolutely new fullness of life, an experience expressed in his exclamation.

The essence of this incident is that the student who was living had really faced death, but he was helped to return again to the living. This greatly transformed his life in the blink of an eye, and he relished his newfound fullness of life. It might be an exaggeration, but we might say that finally he was truly alive.

Of course, falling from the cliff gave the logic of A, non-A, and A the opportunity to unfold, but this alone is not the entirety of the matter. Broadly speaking, when we find ourselves alive again after life having been negated, we have a new sense of ourselves. The words of Zen master Hakuin come to mind in this context:

> O young people, if you hate death, die now;
> if you die once, you will not die again.

In reality we are afraid to die. Anxiety rises up when we think about our death. Perhaps something like this feeling of anxiety contributed to the basic assertion in Christianity that "from nothing God created man." According to Martin Heidegger, humanity's existence is suspended in nothingness. But is this nothingness fully a state of nothingness? By believing in and living the words of Hakuin, let's try to "die" once. Hakuin encourages us by saying that death is not just a nihilistic nothingness. On the contrary, we have the ability to experience the fully perfected true nothingness that solves the problem of our death at its root.

How can we come to die while living? Let's learn by turning to the Buddha's way of life. The Buddha, after leaving home, practiced severe asceticism under Brahmin masters for six years.

Dissatisfied with the results, the Buddha ultimately ended his observation of austerities, regained his health, and entered into deep, silent meditation under the Bodhi tree. He then attained perfect enlightenment at the sight of the morning star. We can say that consequently he found the final solution to the question "What is life?" Since the Buddha proclaimed a middle way between ascetic suffering and indulgence in pleasure, he might be charged with rejecting asceticism entirely. However, for me this is not entirely accurate. Due to the nourishment he acquired as a direct result of severe ascetic practice, the Buddha attained a wonderful state of realization called "supreme enlightenment" (*anuttara-samyak-sambodhi*).

Of course it isn't necessary to practice as much asceticism as the Buddha did. But imagine how it would be to throw oneself into an intense practice wherein one constantly asked with one's whole body and mind, "What is this life?" while still young and healthy. With intense practice, even when you feel that you've reached the furthest extremity of practice and are about to give up and say, "No more," you will have the courage to take one more step, to leap into the void with a defiant cry of determination. In the face of our own Great Death we encounter a new sense of ourselves—a way of being we weren't even aware of until now. To truly experience and live the fullness and true reality of ourselves opens us up to a deep and wonderful state of being.

2

CONSIDER THE MIND

I SEE MANY THINGS when I open my eyes. When I stand in front of a mirror, for example, I see my face reflected in it. I then think, "Here is an image of my face, the reflected image of my face in the mirror, which stands outside of myself." But this is a misunderstanding, because the face that I see is just a shadow in my mind. The mirror, as well as the face that appears in it, are nothing more than pictures that my mind has drawn on the canvas called "my mind." The face in the mirror is but one example. Everything that I recognize is an image constituted by my mind, a picture drawn in my mind.

How does this drawing take place on the canvas of the mind? As I stand before the mirror, my face is reflected in it. The image of my face appears, independent of my will. It will be reflected there, even if I don't want it to be. My will has no involvement in it. A great power is at work here, one that transcends human will. Buddhism recognizes this great power as the force of dependent origination (*pratītya-samutpāda*). Let me explain this in greater detail according to the Buddhist philosophy known as Representation Only (*vijñaptimātra*, also called Mind Only or *cittamātra*): standing before the mirror activates the power of dependent origination, and from seeds that exist deep within the store con-sciousness (ālaya-vijñāna) a sensation called vision sprouts forth. This is how the image of the reflection in the mirror is drawn on the canvas of the mind. When it encounters the bare image of the reflection, thought colors the face that appears there: "Oh! My face has become so old!"

The collaborative actions of three things were needed to draw the image of "my reflected face" on the mind's canvas: sensa-tion, feeling, and language. Even though we may subscribe to the above-described notion of "a single person, a single world," which tells us that one cannot escape the realm of one's own imagination, basic sensations are nonetheless frequently simi-lar between persons without much individual variation. On the other hand, we also know that there can be quite a bit of per-sonal variation in feeling. When viewing cherry blossoms, for instance, some people feel overflowing love and say, "How beau-tiful! How gorgeous!" But others may feel annoyed and say, "I'd prefer to see plum blossoms." Diverse forms of thought emerge based on what is held in the deep layers of the mind. Liking or disliking cherry blossoms is but one example.

The larger issue is to notice that emotions and thoughts color raw sense data. This is particularly true of anger, covetousness, and other such antagonistic emotions. The passionate hatred we feel as soon as we meet someone we dislike, or the passionate craving that we feel at the sight of something we like very much, are both imposed on the raw data of the senses.

In the metaphor of the mind drawing a picture, note that

applying the brush to provide the final touches is the last step in completing a picture. Similarly, the moment we say, "This is X," we have completed the image on the canvas of our mind by naming it. We clearly understand the identified thing to be what we have identified it to be.

Representation Only philosophers observed precisely this sort of complex mental activity and concluded on the basis of their observations that the mind as a whole is comprised of eight types. The Representation Only theory of the eightfold consciousness is articulated as follows:

- five types of sensory consciousness (seeing, hearing, smelling, tasting, touching)
- mental consciousness
- afflicted or ego consciousness (the mind of latent attachment that operates at a deeper level)
- store consciousness (*ālaya-vijñāna*; the "basic" or "source" mind)

The five types of sensory consciousness combine to sketch cognition of the world. Mental consciousness adds a conceptual dimension to this, appending names to fill in the details of the image that allow us to comprehend the various data as this or that "thing." Afflicted consciousness underlies conceptual consciousness and adds further coloration to experience by dividing the perceiver from the perceived and placing the various "things" perceived in relation to the self. By its activation even more "color" is added to the mental illustration of that "thing."

All of these layers of mind emerge from the store consciousness, which is the fundamental or source mind.

We can think of the mind as being like a painter. If we settle the mind and restrain our attention, keeping it focused within, we can silently observe the process whereby the activity of the mind draws and colors in the various "things" of perception. By engaging in this type of inward observation we come to clearly see the principles of Representation Only.

Throughout our lives there are two types or worlds of experience: we experience the waking world and we experience the world of dreams. Suppose that you have just awakened from a dream into the "real" world. Having awakened from the dream and having reflected on it, we say, "Oh, it was a dream. It wasn't real." But are we correct to think this way? What exactly is the difference between the world experienced in dreams and the world experienced in waking life? Isn't this world that I now see with my eyes, hear with my ears, and ponder with my mind the same as the world of dreams in terms of how it is experienced?

We know only these two worlds of waking and dream experience. Given that there are only these two, it seems impossible to determine that one is ultimately more true than the other. This world that we take to be reality certainly also has a sort of dream-like quality because it is also produced by the mind.

Without giving it much thought, I tend to consider my mind as being like a transparent mirror, upon which the outside world is reflected in just the way it exists. But this is absolutely wrong. Everything we experience—whether shapes, colors, or concepts—

are shadows, molded and constructed by my mind. The world I cognize is nothing more than the painting I have made with the various drawing materials available to me in the brush box of my mind. The world does not exist exactly as I cognize it; instead it exists only for me, like an illusion, a dream.

When the great samurai general Oda Nobunaga received the news of the defeat of the vanguard of his army at the battle of Okehazama, distraught, he danced about and sang, "When I think of the fifty years we are given to live here on Earth, it seems like a passing dream. Is there anyone who doesn't soon die after coming into life?" Similarly, Kanpaku Toyotomi Hideyoshi uttered the following lines on his deathbed:

Is not my body like vanishing dew?
The things of Osaka, too, are like a dream of dreams.

We should not think this way only when facing imminent death, but should see this truth here and now, in the very midst of our daily lives. It is very important that we realize this fact that everything we experience as utterly real is actually fantasy—here and now—in the middle of our daily lives. When we realize that everything is a dream, an illusion, without any substance, that there is no fixed and unchanging matter, we become able to finally bring our attachment to things to an end. There are some who, despite realizing that what they cling to is dreamlike, want to make it a wonderful dream nonetheless.

When I say in a lecture, "Everything is like a dream," inevitably some student will meet me after class to complain about how awful it is to think that this life is like a dream. But I ask them in return, "When you consider that we don't remember how we got here, or when this life began, don't you feel like this resembles our experience in dreams?" If they stop to consider this, eventually they acknowledge its truth. The great thing about us human beings is that we are naturally endowed with a sense of awareness that is innately capable of understanding the truth about reality.

Everything we experience is just a conceptual construction in the mind—nothing more. To truly realize that everything is as a dream, essentially we must become a buddha like Śākyamuni, the historical Buddha. The Sanskrit term *buddha* is the past participial form of the verb *budh,* which means "to wake." The epithet *buddha* thus refers to one who has awakened as an enlightened being. When we finally awaken from a long night's wandering in dreams, we realize that they were dreams by comprehending the entirety of the world about whose status we were confused. Our waking consciousness completely swallows the entire world of the dream. The term *buddha* calls us to awaken, as soon as possible, from the suffering of this long night's dream of life.

The mind that we possess is in fact a vast and boundless territory, but we are only aware of a small portion of it, like seeing the tip of an iceberg poking above the water. The quantity of things experienced from the time of our birth until this moment seems nearly infinite and is impossible to recollect. Where do we store all this information, this constantly swelling totality of memory?

As we get up in the morning, the self-centered world immediately breaks into our experience like the Big Bang. The power of its influence works itself into everything we experience. In this world there exist myself, others, nature, and the universe, from the great heavens in which the stars sparkle all the way down to the smallest particles. From where does our mind draw this dormant power, capable of revealing the boundless world?

Humanity has discovered new realities one after the other and has always acquired new knowledge and developed new technologies with each new revelation. We have even deciphered our own genes, and it is almost as if we can manipulate life itself. We have built a space station, and someday human beings will be able to travel through space to live on the moon or on Mars. Where does the potential to realize myriad new things reside?

At the moment we are just ordinary people who live within an illusory world. Young Śākyamuni, too, was an ordinary human like us, but as the result of practice he became the Buddha, an enlightened being. However, it would be more accurate to say that his religious practice was only a condition (*pratyaya*) for his awakening. The cause (*hetu*) for becoming the Buddha already existed in a latent state within Śākyamuni himself. The principal cause for becoming a buddha already exists within our minds. So where, exactly, does the potential to bring about this wonderful act, the capacity to become an enlightened being, actually exist?

Representation Only philosophy claims that all of these powers lie dormant, as seeds within the deepest part of the mind known as the store consciousness. The existence of the store consciousness is not a mere hypothesis arrived at logically. It was discovered by practitioners of yoga who through their yogic practice silenced the superficial mind and delved deep into the internal mind. Let's delve a bit more into the idea of the store consciousness.

"Things" have various attributes. For example, an apple has the attributes of being round in shape and red in color. Although I cognize these types of attributes in the apple, can I really say that these attributes exist in the apple itself, in the external world? Or do the attributes of "shape" and "color" exist in the mind that cognizes them? John Locke, a leading philosopher of British empiricism, divided the qualities of things into primary and secondary. He insisted that primary qualities necessarily exist in objects in the external world and that were it not for these properties we could not conceive of the existence of things at all. The primary qualities he specified are extension, impenetrability, movement and stillness, form, and number. The secondary qualities are properties such as color, sound, smell, and taste, which our senses appropriate.

In the third or fourth century c.e., an intense debate about whether attributes are a part of things themselves or exist internally in our minds developed among Buddhist scholars of India. The Representation Only doctrine supported the view that everything, including attributes, exists in the mind and is the product of the store consciousness.

Eighteenth-century British philosopher George Berkeley's theory seems similar to the theory of Representation Only. Berkeley proposed a theory of subjective idealism, maintaining, in opposition to Locke, that things as such do not exist in the outside world. All that exists, he claimed, are "spirits" (or conscious subjects) and "ideas" in the mind. But Berkeley is quite different than Representation Only philosophers in that he posited the actual existence of God. One of the problems of a perfect idealism is that if everything is an idea in the mind, it becomes difficult to account for the continuing existence of mountains, rivers, and the like when we are not actively perceiving them. To counter this objection, Berkeley surmised that when we are not perceiving nature, the idea of nature still exists in the mind of God.

How does the Representation Only doctrine, which does not recognize a transcendental God, approach this problem? The Representation Only theory emphasizes that the store consciousness simultaneously creates nature and cognizes that created nature. According to this line of thinking, there are two natures: the nature that is apprehended by the eyes and other physical senses, and the nature that is the object of the store consciousness and is continuously cognized deep in the mind by the store consciousness.

Furthermore, the store consciousness does not create and cognize only nature, for it is the fundamental or original mind from which *everything* originates—my body, the things of daily life around me, the mountains and rivers, the stars in the heavens above, all five senses and their respective consciousnesses, and mental consciousness, our thinking mind.

Since the whole of existence is produced from this store

FIGURE 2: THE STORE CONSCIOUSNESS CREATES
EVERYTHING WE KNOW

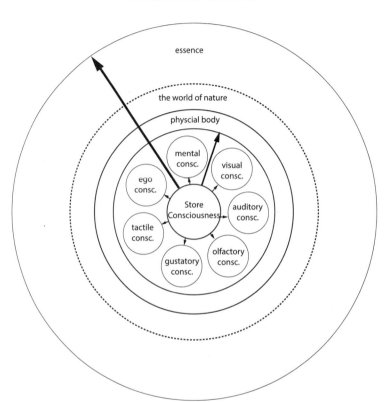

In Buddhism the physical body is thought of as primarily
sensory because it is the means of sensation.

"The world of nature" refers to the perceived environment. According to Representation
Only philosophy, this is merely an abstract, imagined form of nature.

"Essence" refers to the ultimate form of nature that pervades everything
and can only be known with nondiscriminatory wisdom.

consciousness, it is also known as "the consciousness that houses all seeds" (*sarva-bījakam-vijñānam*). Sparing you the detailed explanation, I shall enumerate here in brief the work of the consciousness that houses all seeds.

1. It preserves the fruits of past karma.
2. It gives rise to the whole of our present and future existence.
3. It produces and maintains the physical body.
4. It continuously produces and cognizes nature.
5. It becomes the subject of the cycle of rebirth (*samsara*).

In the following chapters we will examine these points in greater detail.

3 ◦

Consider Karma

Once we begin to hate someone or something, that hate will grow by itself. Encounters with unpleasant things produce feelings of gloom. Human relationships, with all of their inevitable troubles, create stress. All these things happen because the grosser levels of mind deposit effects within the deeper layers of the mind. In other words, our gross thoughts exert karmic influences over us. Advocates of the Representation Only school argue that these karmic influences are planted in the store consciousness. They therefore call these karmic impressions "seeds" (*bīja*).

The karmic seeds we carry within ourselves are responsible for our habits (*vāsanā*), the behaviors we acquire by repeated action or by training. To understand the idea of training, picture a young bird attempting to fly by repeatedly flapping its little wings while watching its mother fly. In just this way, residual feelings and traces of repeated actions are impressed upon the deepest layers of the mind, where they form seeds—the bases of our engrained habits. Here is another example: a technique used to keep a suit smelling fresh is to place a sachet of herbs in the pocket. The pleasant aroma of the herbs gradually permeates the whole suit. Likewise, recurring actions of our gross mind

◦

slowly permeate the deep layers of the mind, leaving behind lingering traces that become habits. Our thoughts and actions imbue habits.

Scientists speak of the law of conservation of mass. Buddhist philosophers similarly have a law of inextinguishable karma. The gist of this law is that human activity, the karmic energy in each moment, will not be extinguished. Instead, it accumulates in the store consciousness, like a form of potential energy. This stored potential can be good, like clear water, or bad, like murky water. More and more, as our life goes on, our habitual attachment to ourselves and the impure mental states produced by this attachment contaminate the store consciousness. Therefore we continue to hate others in our thoughts, without appreciating the contaminating effect this has on our own consciousness. When we plot something wicked in our minds, we think it is fine so long as nobody knows about it. Some religious people discourage even wicked thoughts because they believe God is always watching.

Although in Japan we say, "The Buddha will forgive you until the third time," the doctrine of the store consciousness says that we never escape the effects of our thoughts, whether it is the first or the third time we have thought them. The karma of thought will still defile the deep layer of our minds. The store consciousness is not like a bamboo basket; a thought that comes into the store consciousness can not ever come back out. It does not overlook any karmic seeds but retains them all.

There is a bright side to this idea as well. This type of thinking also draws our attention to the wonderful quality of good karma.

○ ···

It teaches us that each moment's effort, each day's diligence, will undoubtedly bear wonderful fruits. The seeds planted in the store consciousness will grow and develop, and when the proper conditions are in place and the occasion is right, they will blossom forth. Therefore, we should cultivate good and pure seeds, provide them with constant nourishment, and eradicate those bad, defiled seeds that have been planted deep in the store consciousness.

Thoughts and actions at the surface level of our mind necessarily leave impressions or plant seeds deep within the mind of the store consciousness. In the future, these seeds will sprout and bloom, in turn, into that outer mind. This ongoing series of causes and effects forms a cycle in the mind, which we call "dependent origination from the store consciousness" (*ālaya-vijñāna-pratītya-samutpāda*). This complex term is not meant to be just a piece of technical jargon that we learn to throw around. It is actually an important ethical principle. We should spend some time reflecting on the way in which our superficial thoughts and actions leave impressions in the deeper layers of our unconscious selves and then bubble up again to affect how we think and act later. We must understand that the mind does indeed work according to this principle of dependent origination. This simple insight becomes the basis for real personal transformation in our daily lives.

I am convinced of the truth of the theory of "a single person, a single world"—everything in my perceptible universe is the product of my own mind. For example, when I hear a Beethoven symphony, I am aware of the fact that I am reproducing the music in my mind according to the musicians' performance of it. We tend to think of ourselves as blank slates when it comes to perception. We hear sounds from the outside world and imagine that they are being printed upon our minds from the outside, like an image being drawn on paper. The truth is nothing like that. The tune that I hear with the help of my ear is actually uniquely mine. Only I hear this particular version of the tune the way I hear it. My own listening is uniquely shaped by my own prior habits of listening. It's true that the sound of the song in the external world is objectively just one, but on the basis of this external sound each person produces their own unique subjective experience of it. So while we nominally listen to the same performance, we cannot truly hear it exactly in the same subjective way. When the concert is over, we say to each other, "That was wonderful!" We may all agree with one another, but each one of us has actually had a unique experience of the performance, colored in slightly different ways according to many conditions in our minds.

This truth regarding experience can be applied equally to all of our senses. We are constantly creating a world of experience that is unique to ourselves. From one perspective, I feel like I am just a tiny, insignificant being in this boundless universe. But when I think about the miracle of the uniqueness of individual experience, I see that I am a wondrous being with the ability to produce everything in my universe.

When gazing at the stars in the immense night sky, for example, I am amazed to think that light emitted from the Andromeda galaxy two million years ago is striking my eye. I am overcome by excitement and wonder. But we should really look at ourselves with that same feeling of amazement. We ourselves have the power to reproduce, in our minds the image of the Andromeda galaxy two million light years away. Doesn't this power make you feel that human beings are a wondrous thing, that our existence is amazing? Let's put a stop to the kind of judgmental meanness that leads us to think of ourselves as mundane or worthless. We ourselves are capable of reproducing everything we encounter in the field of our perception—and this is really wonderful.

To be sure, the actions and effects of others do exist apart from ourselves in the external world. An inspiring book about music—Roman Lawrence's *The Life of Beethoven*, for example—will invariably move readers when they read it. The events in Beethoven's biography happened long before I even existed. The conjunction of knowing about Beethoven's struggle to compose the Ninth Symphony and the efforts of the orchestra and chorus to perform it at a concert allows me to re-manifest a fully appreciated Ninth Symphony in my mind.

It was only possible for me to have my own experience of the symphony because various other people worked to produce the event. These circumstances outside of ourselves that contribute to our experience constitute what is referred to as "cooperating conditions" (*adhipati-pratyaya*). So we must be thankful for the efforts of others that help to realize the effect of our experiences. But, in an ultimate sense, the power to reproduce the Ninth Symphony in my personal experience is what really makes my hearing the symphony possible. This, too, is quite wonderful when you think about it.

I recently saw an article in a newspaper that contained an image of an area of the universe that is 12.2 billion light years away. It is quite exciting to see an image of a part of our universe as it existed 12.2 billion light years ago. Scientists looking at background radiation are hoping soon to capture an image of the universe just after the Big Bang, too. What does it mean for our lives, if we manage to capture these types of pictures?

First, humanity will have become capable of capturing the image of the origin of the present universe. The universe we see around us is a complexly differentiated world. Looking just at the earth, we detect living beings, mountains and rivers, earth and sky. Above us, an infinite number of galaxies are scattered across this unimaginably gigantic void of space. This is a world of complex and boundless differentiation.

But this picture of an incredibly distant past, just after the Big Bang, will show us the origins of this complex and differentiated world. Instead of complexity and differentiation, we may see a universe that was rather uniform and equal. We may come to better understand what originally existed prior to all this differentiation. On top of any discoveries we may make about the origin of the universe, we will also be discovering something about humanity: we are capable, as creatures that live in this universe, of replaying or re-manifesting an image of the universe when it began.

Consider this: what happened billions of years ago no longer exists in the present moment. So what does it mean to say that we see the birth of the universe in this present moment? Light emitted billions of years ago travels through space over vast periods of time until it strikes my eyes, where the stimulus of light is transduced into electrochemical signals at the retina and passed along to the brain, where, at last, the signals are reconstituted into an image of the universe in the past. The light that is the original source for the image of the universe in my mind may have come from outside to interact with my eyes at the end of its long journey, but if I myself did not possess the power to re-manifest the image that the light creates, the image of the past universe would never appear to my mind. It is truly amazing that we are equipped with the ability to do this.

So we can think of human beings as having the potency to generate everything. Next, let's consider the importance of this term *everything*. As mentioned above, the store consciousness is also referred to as the consciousness that houses all seeds. Just as planted seeds sprout and develop trunks, branches, leaves, and fruit, impressions left in our basic, unconscious mind bear a latent, generative potential to bring forth all sorts of experience as their fruit. This is why Buddhist teachings often compare the mind to a "field" and refer to thoughts and actions as "seeds," and why the mind is said to have the power to produce everything we experience. This idea may be strange and hard to make sense of when approached from a Christian perspective. I suspect that teachings that presuppose the existence of a transcendent God, one that exists apart from human life, would have great difficulty supporting this kind of view.

Of course, there may be a world outside of me, but it is none-theless the case that everything that I experience, know, and think about is generated within my own mind. They are images drawn by my own mind. The image of the universe 12.2 billion years ago is no different. The production of this image depends on the external stimulus gained via telescope, but I must already have the capacity to produce the image within my own mind in order for it to be realized. Where did this capacity come from? According to the Representation Only doctrine, this capacity was latent as a *seed* in the store consciousness. Contemporary astronomy continues to observe by facing outward. However, we should not forget the fact that this outward observation is but one factor in our perception. It is what Buddhists call a "cooperating cause." Beyond this, we must also consider the *original cause*, which is to say the potential latent in the deep mind, which, when charged by that stimulus, blossoms forth.

This power of our mind is amazing, but it is also dreadful. Why is it dreadful? The power of our mind is dreadful because it has also made possible the conception and production of weapons of mass destruction, like atomic bombs. With our rapidly advancing knowledge of the DNA that makes up our genes, we have nearly attained the ability to manipulate life and create human beings by cloning. So while the creative mind is wonderful, it can also be terrible. It is important that we learn to understand how to use this mind responsibly and with care, as I will discuss below.

○ ···

4.

Ego

IT IS IMPOSSIBLE to find someone without self-consciousness, without a sense of "I" or "my." We look at our hand and immediately think "my hand"; we open our eyes and immediately think "I see." As soon as I realize that others are fooling me, I angrily think, "I am being fooled!"

From this perspective, the Sanskrit concept of "no self" (*anātman*), a fundamental point of Buddhist doctrine, is not so much a matter of faith as it is an objective fact. Buddhism does not ask us to believe in and become "no self." Rather, it encourages us to think about and recognize that we already are this "no self." Even though we do not exist as the selves we imagine ourselves to be, we insist on living according to the notions of "I," "self," "my," and so on.

It is easy to recognize our self-consciousness in an ordinary sense. When we face an audience, for example, we become tense and much more aware of ourselves. As soon as the train approaches the platform, I begin to think of myself, rushing to secure a seat for myself. If I am successful, I experience self-consciousness in the form of pride and the knowledge that I excel at my discipline. There is no limit to these sorts of ordinary experiences of self-consciousness.

So why do we adhere to this idea of ourselves and become so attached to it? The Representation Only doctrine posits a distinct part of our consciousness called "ego consciousness" (*manonāma-vijñāna*) that is the cause of this habitual tendency. Ego consciousness is defined as the aspect of the mind that is constantly self-attached; it faces inwards, as if it were repeatedly thinking "me, me." This is always the case. Whether we are sleeping or awake, it is always running, for as long as we circulate through the cycle of birth and death.

If this tenacious and persevering aspect of mind did not exist, there would be no cause to think "I," "my," "myself" as we encounter the external world. Whatever we do, whatever we think, this "self" comes and goes with it, like the constant appearance and vanishing of bubbles in a kettle of boiling water. Ego consciousness is just like boiling water and thoughts of "I" and "my" are like the bubbles.

It usually isn't possible to perceive the working of the ego consciousness. Like the store consciousness, it is an aspect of the mind that operates subconsciously at a very deep level. But we can infer the work of the ego consciousness beneath awareness because we can notice the pervasive insistence on ourselves in the course of our actions.

What is the object that the ego consciousness refers to when it thinks "I" or "my"? When we observe our hand or face or our own thoughts, this part of the mind projects the idea of a "self" that underlies "my hand," "my face," and even "my mind." Eventually, this ego consciousness naturally and consistently takes as its object the entire complex of the body and the mind.

According to the Representation Only doctrine, this body-mind complex is really the wrong object. The body and mind can be known tangibly, but there is a more fundamental object that we only discover through the practice of yogic meditation. That true object is nothing other than the store consciousness. Earlier forms of Buddhist doctrine posited that the object that our minds take to be the "self" is nothing other than the five aggregates, or the five real component parts that make up the mind-body complex. But the Representation Only doctrine posits that the ego consciousness does not take the five aggregates as its object but instead takes the store consciousness as its object. The ego consciousness takes the store consciousness and construes it as the self. This position indicates the significant philosophical developments that the Representation Only doctrine made as a result of their investigations into consciousness.

It is easy to say that the ego consciousness takes the store consciousness as its object. But as we are talking about something that occurs very deep within the mind, which makes it very hard for us to truly understand. In order to comprehend this fact, we must delve deeply into ourselves to conduct a careful and precise investigation. Even then, it is not at all easy to clearly recognize the activity of the ego consciousness.

Our examination must make use of the concentration attained through the practice of yogic meditation. We must silence the workings of the senses of touch and vision, and concentrate on the breath. If we do just this, a new world will gradually emerge—the deep regions of the mind will begin to manifest themselves. The second that this power of concentration is interrupted, the old consciousness of our selves rushes back in. The object of the "self" manifests as soon as our deep mind bends back on itself, producing a sort of echo of itself. Though we may not be directly aware of the ego consciousness, we can certainly read and learn about it. This is how we take the first step towards undoing our attachment to ourselves, which tortures us and others as well.

We know how big our bodies are. I am five feet, seven inches tall, and I weigh 155 pounds. But how big is my mind? Fundamentally, the mind has no form or color, and no extension in space—so how can we even begin to answer this question? Nonetheless, we speak of body and mind, matter and spirit, and we try to compare these two as if they were things of the same dimension. This is the source of a great problem.

For example, Descartes proposed a theory of body-mind parallelism that regarded body and mind as two different substances with the respective qualities of extension, or *res extensa* in Latin, and cognition, or *res cogitans*. But what do we gain by settling the matter so easily? If these two are independent substances, does the mind exist inside the body? Or, on the contrary, does the body exist within the mind? Or do they both exist in different places?

Some people may support a theory of "brain only," which would be different from the Mind Only doctrine. A "brain only" position would argue that the mind is nothing more than a function of the cerebrum and other physical components of the brain. Since the cerebrum is a part of the body we automatically start thinking that the mind exists inside the body. But take the case of eyesight: it would be absurd to suggest that because I now see my hands, I should think that my hand exists within my vision. Could we not also think of the mind jumping from the cerebrum and seeing the hand? This type of thinking creates a lot of confusion and we end up not understanding anything anymore. Therefore let's try to think more deeply.

When I see Mount Fuji, I think it is big and tall. At that moment, if we calmly observe the mind, we realize that the great mountain has already entered into that aspect of the mind that we call "eyesight." Consequently, in order to contain Mt. Fuji, the mind becomes bigger than Mount Fuji. Certainly what we are talking about is nothing other than an image of the mountain in my mind. There may be people insisting on the contrary: that the mind is small and Mount Fuji, out there, is big. In reality nobody has seen Mount Fuji *itself* since the physical mountain is external to anyone's mind. So does this real, physical Mount Fuji, 3,776 meters tall, actually exist?

This deepens the confusion. We need to slow down and reconsider. Let's be sure of the following two facts. First, as already mentioned, the mind has no extension, no "bigness" to it. The mind is not a spatial thing, and it is a mistake to argue about the mind's existence inside or outside of the body. Second, everything, taken as it is, greatly exceeds the limits of our language and logic. Therefore to speak about the mind as such in language is in the end impossible. The only way in which we can come to know about a thing is by becoming one with it ourselves—in other words, by experiencing it. This is why we can only know heat or cold by experiencing it, not by having it explained to us in terms of physics or anything else.

The great Kobe earthquake of 1995 was a truly tragic event in the recent past. What must it have felt like to lose family and friends, to be the victims of a fire that reduced everything to ash? It was a tragedy beyond imagination. But human beings are endowed with wonderful energy. The effort to rebuild the affected area has progressed far. Human beings have the power to face harsh realities and to reshape them. Perhaps we can also define human beings as beings uniquely endowed with the will, wisdom, and motivational power to accept facts as facts, to discern and clarify them, and then to overcome them by constructing a new reality.

In his *Pensées*, Pascal declares, "The greatness of man is that he knows himself to be miserable. A tree does not know itself to be miserable. It is then being miserable to know oneself to be miserable; but it is also being great to know that one is miserable." Reading Pascal in the light of Buddhism, we can supply a name for this ability of ours to know that we are miserable: Buddhists call it *prajñā*, a Sanskrit term that means "wisdom." Some scholars might object, insisting that *prajñā* has nothing to do with something as shallow and superficial as this. But I rebuff such objections! What Pascal is speaking about is the wonderful capacity that we have within ourselves to objectively consider the self, to look directly into the self without turning away from it—sometimes admiring it, occasionally being critical, introspective, or repenting with regard to it.

There is a Buddhist practice of yogic meditation that unflinchingly looks at the stark reality of human existence, called "cultivating awareness of impurity" (aśubha-bhāvanā). This practice is used to sever attachment to one's body and eventually to the idea of the self. The Japanese developed a version of this practice known as "The Nine Stage Picture of Ono no Komachi." This method of meditation involves contemplating a set of nine pictures that depict the gradual decomposition of the body of Komachi, a peerless beauty. As one practices, one relates one's own situation to that of Komachi.

The prospect of a ghost in a dark and creaky attic is frightening. The self that fears things like ghosts in the darkness is just as mysterious as a ghost itself. Before being afraid of ghosts that may lurk in darkness, let's think about something ghastly that lies closer at hand—our own bodies. We are built on bones. It is terrifying to think of a skull appearing before one's eyes. But are we not also carrying around skulls in our heads? It seems attractive when covered with flesh, but even the most beautiful person becomes terrifying and repulsive when the flesh is peeled away from the bone. We may not necessarily need these sorts of images in order to develop an attitude of detachment, but they are certainly powerful aids in bringing such an attitude about.

To walk through the practice, we begin by simply taking a step away from ourselves and looking back at ourselves objectively. We observe our bodies with the thought, "It's made up of bones, blood, pus, and other impure things." As we contemplate the body in this way, we gradually become aware that we are standing a bit apart from ourselves, one part of us observing the other. It is frightening to think of ourselves as skeletons, to imagine the bones and gristle underneath, but it is certain that one day my flesh will rot away and the bones that are really there will be revealed.

It is important not to end our contemplation when we encounter the shock of seeing ourselves as nothing more than bones. We must take our thought to the next level. It is also important to be aware that for each of us there is a "self," apart from the body we identify with, who is observing it.

The spotlight of awareness is not just shining on the picture of us made up of bones, it also shines on that part of ourselves that observes it. We must illumine that aspect of ourselves that is aware of ourselves. So it is a two-step process: we become aware that we are seeing ourselves as made up of disgusting substances, and then we give the spotlight one more inward turn to be aware that we are aware of seeing ourselves in that way. It's easy to see how complicated the simple idea of "being aware" becomes!

You can experiment with this "spotlight" yourself, rotating it within yourself until you too come to understand self-awareness. Strictly speaking, we could go on like this forever. There are not just a few layers to self-awareness, but infinitely more that follow the same pattern: one more self, one more self aware of that one behind it, and another behind that, and so on. The deeper we delve into ourselves, the deeper we find the mind to be. We begin with something striking, like awareness of the impurity of our bodies, which allows us to step back from ourselves and see ourselves seeing ourselves. From there we can quickly see that the mind is quite deep.

Now let's get back to thinking about the mind. We already considered that the human being is constituted of body and mind. It is easy to become aware of the existence of the body. Simply open your eyes and you will see your hand—there it is! Simply stand in front of a mirror and you will see your face reflected in it.

So how do we conceive of the existence of the mind? As already stated above, the mind has no form, color, or spatial extension. It is rather difficult to grasp its existence. Of course, we may speak of it as if it were otherwise: "Give due care to the mind," or "The twenty-first century is the era of the mind." But such statements are just wordplay until we resolve the underlying question of what exactly the mind is.

Let's take a moment to discuss this. First, we might analyze the mind into the following three parts:

Sensation

Emotion

Thought

So we see three components of the mind: sensation, emotion, and thought. Sensation provides the basic data derived from perceiving the world. This aspect of the mind retains the minimum data needed to reconstruct time and space and the events happening in them. We know of course that individual minds can vary significantly from one to another, but there may not be much individual variation with regard to sensation.

The problems start with the second component, emotion. It is here that our ego consciousness comes rather strongly into play. The bright sunny day becomes a gloomy day for a sad person. The world in which we live becomes painful or pleasing, bright or dark, depending on the color of an individual's emotions.

The third component, thought, will also vary greatly from person to person. Our world can be completely transformed, depending on the thoughts and words we use to make sense of our encounters with it. Somebody points out another person's defects and they may react violently: "Damn it! You like to make fun of my weak points!" Another person might accept the same with gratitude: "Thank you for letting me know! I want to change that about myself."

Language is a wonderful thing that has a power of its own. If I say something I do not mean, I may still be influenced by those words, and even convince myself of them. The thinking mind is different for each person, but the question remains: is it possible to think in a universal way, without being influenced by our individual ego consciousness? Is there a correct language and valid logic with respect to thought? Is thinking entirely about language?

Ordinarily, when we think about something we think using language, using concepts and logic. This is how we would typically define the act of thinking. But if we accept the premise that human beings are capable of comprehending absolute truth, then we must also accept that thinking cannot be fully defined in terms of language. This is because language is only capable of expressing absolute truth in abstract terms, rather than directly. You might say that language really serves up a metaphorical grasp of reality. Language helps us to speak about reality in terms of something else. This applies equally to all words, since the word is always different from the thing it points to. All language is metaphor.

The problem is that, without reflection, we habitually convince ourselves that things exist in the way that we speak and think of them. It's easy to think, "I am living in this world; I exist in this world." But what do words like *I*, *world*, and *exist*, actually indicate? It is futile to search for an answer to this question within the bounds of language, because no matter how much we search we will still be speaking about what we are searching for. So what should we do?

There is only one thing to do: we must think apart from language, by becoming the thing as such. The ideal and ultimate form of thought is done not with an egoistic mind, but with a truly mature mind—a mind that becomes one with its object.

FIGURE 3: THOUGHT

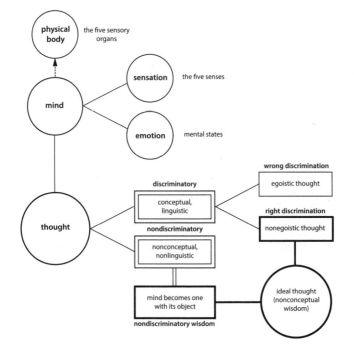

The physical body consists of the five sensory organs, namely, eye, ear, nose, tongue, and body.

The five senses are our awareness of what the five sensory organs encounter.

Mental states are the subtle mental activities that accompany the mind itself and color its experience.

5

THINGS OUTSIDE THE MIND

WE HAVE ALL SORTS of desires. The very energy of life wells up from our desires, our thinking, "I have to do this," or "I need that." But the deepening of desire, its transformation into attachment, produces suffering. The suffering that attachment produces is not merely abstract, it can also drag us into crime and sin. We desire things, sex, fame, and so on. I want to be promoted at work; I want to live in a beautiful house; I want to attract a beautiful mate; and I need money to do these things. When I am successful and win a beautiful mate, I then suffer with worry that my success will fade and I'll lose my lover.

All of these objects—a house, money, a man or woman, a career—are ideas articulated through language, and we all consider them to be real. In other words, we think that these things substantially exist. Thoughts by themselves may not be harmful, but problems arise when my thoughts about these things become attachments to them.

Do things really exist as our thoughts and words suggest they do? For example, take the simple statement, "Here is a pencil." When we investigate this judgment, we find that it entails thinking, "This pencil exists as a substantially different thing from me." But do things really exist in this way, the way they are thought of in words? Is there no mistake in this simple thinking? Of course, there may be something that corresponds to a pencil in the outside world, but what we can say exists with complete surety is the image of a pencil. When I concentrate on that image, I'm unable to say that it is actually a pencil. Instead, what I feel safe to say is, "It is precisely the image of a pencil—just that." Originally it is devoid of name; it is something unattainable by language. It is "just that."

On the other hand, when I ask myself about this image of a pencil, specifically referring to it as a "pencil," it immediately becomes a real pencil to me. In other words, once I refer to it as a pencil it becomes for me a real thing that exists outside of my

FIGURE 4. THE PROCESS OF THE FORMATION OF THINGS

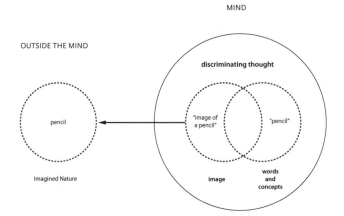

Discriminatory thought conflates words and concepts with images in the mind, thereby creating the illusion of substantially real objects separate from our knowledge of them.

mind. But the word pencil and the image of a pencil are absolutely different things. When a word for a thing and an image of a thing intermingle, they suggest an established, substantial thing in the outside world. But it is merely imagined to have this nature.

This is all well and good, because it would be impossible to live in the world without establishing various things in this way. To cook food, to prepare miso soup, for example, I need vegetables such as radish and onion, tofu, bean paste, and a pot for boiling water. In order to procure or ask for these things, it helps to have them established as things in the world. The real problem lies in my attachment to these things that I imagine to be substantially real. The truth is that these things, the substantial, independent existence of which is uncertain, mislead us and we develop attachment to them. Just as a person lost in the desert for many days craves water to cool his throat, we crave money, rank, and much else that we think will satisfy our desires.

So what really exists? This is a serious question. We can only begin to form an answer to it by turning our minds inward and quietly contemplating it. We must try to observe naked and raw existence, by observing what's there before we've attached names or concepts to it.

The major reformation of the mind will not occur by learning things or through accumulating wisdom by reading books. In fact, the opposite is true. Increasing the amount of knowledge and information the mind has to deal with only adds to the agitation and confusion of the mind we seek to dispel. Things in

.... ○

themselves, apart from the conceptual web of language, are simple. They are simple until human beings complicate them with intellectual discrimination, with words and thought. So we must reflect on the limitation and obscuration that language brings.

If we want to step beyond the life of words and inquire into the true reality behind them, language suddenly becomes an obstacle. By making judgments about things being "this" or "that," I grasp at them as something totally different from what they are nakedly, in and of themselves. I actually push myself further away from the reality of whatever it is that precedes and allows me to make judgments about it.

It may be a bit of an exaggeration, but these days I feel that I can only call a pencil "a pencil" after apologizing to it. "I'm sorry, Mr. Pencil, but please allow me to call you a pencil now!" Though we speak of a thing as it really is, the thing as it is is entirely unattainable through words. There is no judgment attached to things as they are.

Thinking about the way in which words cannot convey the reality of things as they really are reveals the limits of discursive thought. We too easily take it for granted that things exist exactly as we speak or think about them, and then we become attached to the things we speak and think about. In the end language and thought traps us.

The most critical problem, in this respect, are the words and ideas *is* and *is not*. The fundamental cause of delusion and suffering is our habit of thinking in terms of "is" and "is not." Things do not exist in the way in which we conceive of them in words and thought. When we recognize and are convinced of this fact, the world begins to drastically change. It suddenly seems possible to live more freely, in a world we haven't yet encountered.

Recently I had a chance to visit China. When I last visited Suzhou six years ago, the city's modern development had just begun. This time I was astounded at how the city had been transformed. The five-story pagoda of the Hanshan temple, which had been under repair on my last visit, had been completed. The view of Suzhou city from the top of the pagoda was drastically different. Not even a hint of Suzhou's former reputation as "the Venice of the Orient" remained. The greenery had dwindled; many new buildings surround the pagoda. The construction boom was even more intense in Shanghai. The height and number of buildings didn't just rival those in Tokyo, they far surpassed them.

I sometimes think about the changes that such developments might create in the minds of the people who live in the city. They live amid the constant influence of department stores, name-brand products, electrical goods, money, and so on, all vying to attract their attention. Amid the economic boom it is easier and easier for a person's mind to be drawn to desirable things. Attachment to things will dry up the mind. The craving caused by attachment grows ever larger, as does its master, the "self." The sense of self and craving are intertwined. Out of the intertwining of these two burst, in turn, department stores, name-brand products, electrical goods, money, and so on.

We need money to live. This is an unavoidable fact. But if we aren't careful, we easily slip into a logic of "I have one but could have two; I have two but could have three." This type of thinking is greed, which along with anger and ignorance is considered a "poison" in Buddhism. In Buddhist teachings greed is compared to water, because, like water, it permeates wherever it can and seeps into everything. Craving is unlimited and boundless. In the midst of a flourishing economic boom, there are even more opportunities for craving to grow. So what is the best thing to do? A principle of Buddhist doctrine contains a hint for us.

This principle is the idea that a bodhisattva gathers wealth through work and business, performed according to right reason, and uses it with measure. The bodhisattva also uses their wealth to provide for others. In this way the bodhisattva benefits both himself or herself and others. One must rightly discern the amount to be used for oneself, without excess, and commit the rest to the salvation of others. That is the rule of the life of the bodhisattva. Is this not precisely the type of stringent admonition we modern people need? By placing our focus on others rather than on the self, we begin to relate to others with a concern for their happiness that is even greater than our concern for ourselves. Money becomes a means and a measure for the happiness of others.

It is foolish to think that we can remove the impurities that pollute our minds by cleaning the outside world. We can only purify our minds with our minds themselves. Understanding this, we must think of ways and means of cleaning the mind. In fact, one of the means of purifying the mind, paradoxically, is to clean the world around us. Typically when we sweep the dust in a room, we assume that the dust is apart from us. But considering what we have learned about the way in which we normally relate to things, dust in the world is dust in the mind. Knowing this fact, we realize how nice it is to clean the room. As the room becomes clean, the mind becomes clean too.

FIGURE 5. THE RESTRAINTS OF LANGUAGE

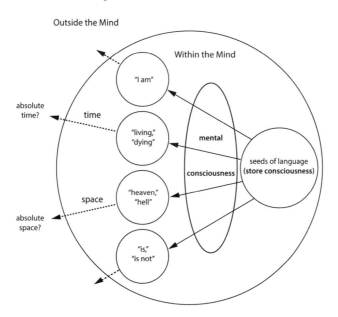

Outside the Mind

Within the Mind

"I am"

absolute time?

time

"living," "dying"

mental

seeds of language (store consciousness)

consciousness

"heaven," "hell"

space

absolute space?

"is," "is not"

The seeds of language and concepts are carried in the store consciousness.

Mental consciousness activates the seeds of language, drawing out words and concepts to think conceptually about the world.

"I am," "living," "heaven," "hell," "is," and "is not" are thus merely words and concepts projected by the mind onto the world outside the mind.

Over the past three years I have taken my students around campus to pick up cigarette butts during the noon break. Usually we would pick up around 500 cigarette butts in the thirty minutes or so we spent each day. Initially my students felt a bit embarrassed to be seen by their peers picking up the cigarette butts when most others were relaxing and hanging out on the campus grounds. However, over the course of a year their self-consciousness gradually diminished and they began to perform the task without any concern, as if nonconceptual wisdom had truly been awakened within them.

If we consider the matter in light of Representation Only doctrine, we could say that each of the students was really cleaning up the world in their minds. The deed is not merely an act that benefits others by cleaning up the campus for them; it is also an occasion to purify one's own mind. Who knows? Maybe it will also give people the idea to stop throwing their cigarette butts on the campus!

Not only trash, but nature itself exists in the mind of each person. It is common to hear the following objection against the point of Representation Only doctrine that states that there is nothing external: if trash exists only in the mind, what happens when someone throws that trash away? Does discarded trash exist only in the mind of the person who threw it away? Is there no trash, no impurity or pollution, that is shared in common by all? This is a legitimate contention.

In response, the Representation Only school contends that nature and things are produced by all together. Everything that is generated by the mind can be separated into things that pertain only to oneself and things shared in common with others. The former refers to the body, and the latter to nature and things.

○ ···

Consequently, mountains, rivers, trash, and the like are things produced by all human beings in common. We all experience them in common. Our attitude toward nature and trash changes when we understand things in this way. We become aware that these things already exist in the mind.

6

NATURE

THE MIND IS NOT like a calm and pure mirror that reflects things just as they are. To illustrate this, consider how we perceive a falling object. Without any reflection, we think that we have seen something outside of ourselves fall. But upon reflection, recalling the principle of "a single person, a single world," we understand that we cannot get outside of our own minds. What we perceive to be a falling object is just the image of a falling object in our minds. Scientifically speaking, falling objects fall in accordance with the law of gravity. But from the point of view of Representation Only philosophy, the law of gravity doesn't contradict the fact that the falling object exists only within the mind.

We can know the law of gravity in two ways: we can observe an object outside of ourselves falling, or we ourselves can fall. How do these two differ? In the first case we observe the image of a falling object in our minds. In the second case we become one with falling itself—we fall. In the first case the thing falling is imagined to be separate from us, whereas in the second case we experience no such separation. We could draw a diagram of an object that is separate from ourselves falling. But we couldn't do the same with respect to directly experiencing falling. Why is this? Because when we directly experience falling, we become one with it—no distinction can be made between subject and object. There is no space between the two. In order to diagram the personal experience of falling, we have to imagine ourselves falling from the outside. That is, we have to break the experience into subject and object.

The Representation Only doctrine contends that whatever we can know is necessarily only consciousness, and therefore we cannot really know an external environment. But even if we believe that external things do exist, we still have to establish just how the human mind is able to perceive the laws by which external things operate. That is, how do we, whose experience is uniquely our own, internalize something that is not uniquely our own? Let's puzzle this out with respect to the law of gravity.

There are two kinds of gravitational force that we can know: a conceptually represented gravitational force, which is not the gravitational force as such, and a gravitational force experienced uniformly with body and mind, which cannot be symbolically represented. It is quite different to conceptually know the law of gravity and to know gravity as it is. The conceptually represented law of gravity is not gravity as it is, because it has been colored, symbolized, and numerically rendered in order for human beings to comprehend it. The "coloring" of gravity comes from our own side. There is no concept of gravity existing "out there" because this symbolic representation is a form of thought. In this way we can say that the laws of physics exist in the mind.

The two greatest achievements of twentieth-century physics

have been the establishment of quantum theory and the theory of relativity. The advent of quantum physics not only revolutionized our conception of matter, it changed our very vision of the world itself. We discovered that the most elementary particles from which matter is formed are far different in their form and behavior than classical physics had led us to believe. After much experimentation and debate, for example, we have come to the conclusion that electrons (and light) bear the characteristics of both a particle and a wave. How can we explain the co-existence of these two sets of characteristics?

One way of explaining it says that human understanding depends upon categories that are fixed and already given, and that it is impossible to understand something without applying one or another of these categories. Thus in the case of light or electrons, although fundamentally they are neither particles nor waves, humans cannot but perceive them in terms of being either particles or waves, because these are categories within our ability to perceive and understand. From this point of view we can say that the way things exist is comprised of both their natural way of being and the way they are perceived to be. These two aspects of a thing's way of being are blended in cognition. The categories that we conceive of to make sense of the world mold the world in their image. It's easy to understand this with a bit of reflection.

But some people say that we perceive things clearly, just as they are. This way of explaining the coexistence of contradictory features supposes that when we perceive things, we are able to step back from existence to know it just as it is, without tainting our knowledge of it with our own perspective. In other words, this way of thinking supposes a perspectiveless knowledge of existence, untainted by being specifically situated in space and time in relation to what is known. This sort of view was consonant with Newton's classical dynamics, but contemporary quantum theory does not accept it.

There is a principle in quantum physics called "the uncertainty principle" or "the principle of indeterminism." This principle says that while in the general world we can simultaneously measure the speed and the position of a thing, in the case of electrons and other very small particles it is impossible to simultaneously determine speed and position. When we determine the speed of a quantum particle, its position automatically becomes indeterminate. This is the gist of Heisenberg's well-known "uncertainty principle." At the atomic level many things happen that transcend our commonsense notions about the world in which we live our daily lives. Taking these observations into consideration, we can say that we human beings do not passively observe existence as it is, but participate in making it as it is.

We may have thought of ourselves, until now, as observers who stand back from existence to observe it objectively, as it is. But now we know that reality is not like that. The fact is, we are participants in the reality we perceive. We ourselves and the existence we perceive form a single set. It isn't advisable, of course, to take these aspects of quantum theory and consider them to be identical to aspects of Representation Only philosophy. However, taking seriously the discoveries that quantum theory have made about reality, we can feel a bit more confident that Representation Only philosophy is not absolutely arbitrary.

When I say that mountains, rivers, and nature itself exist in the mind, nearly everyone will object and tell me how foolish this is. Nature, the phenomenal world, comprised of atoms and molecules, exists outside of me. This isn't just common sense, but the view of the physical sciences. But even if I admit that there is an outside world, since I cannot slip out of my mind in order to know the outside world, I cannot know external nature just as it is. The tangible nature that I see is only an image in my mind.

Now I am looking at a tree. The image of that tree is the object of vision. The image vanishes as I close my eyes, yet in my mind I still think that the tree exists, even though I cannot see it. Representation Only philosophy, however, insists that it doesn't; the tree and the mind that cognizes or doesn't cognize it are both generated within the store consciousness. When we calm our disturbed minds and close our eyes, in absolute tranquility, we don't see or hear anything. But when I do this, I still feel that I exist. This existential awareness feels like essential, raw being. It is unlike the kind of existence I feel by opening my eyes and ears to see and hear a world outside myself. When we calm all of our superficial senses, we delve into the deeper realms of the mind. Sinking deeper and deeper into the mind, until we reach the region of the store consciousness, we come to know the source that simultaneously produces and cognizes things.

Classical mechanics, up until and including Newton's mechanics, proposed that atoms and molecules exist with some extension outside of me. Quantum theory and quantum mechanics taught us that our own existence participates in the existence of things. The Representation Only philosophy tells us that nature, as we perceive it—the nature that we encounter through sensation and color with feelings and words—is not the only nature. Nature also exists in our minds as the object of the store consciousness. These two insights suggest a revolution in our way of viewing nature. There is no doubt that we need political, economic, and social reforms in order to prevent the destruction of nature, but it is also very important that we transform our basic vision of nature.

We need to do more than recite slogans about being kind to nature. We need to first settle, on a very fundamental level, how we view nature. By reflecting on how intimately we ourselves are intertwined with the nature that we perceive, we will come to feel much more closely related to nature. Wouldn't this way of thinking be beneficial to the world? Once we begin to settle more clearly just what this world we live in is, we can begin to ask ourselves how we ought to live in it.

○ ···

II. How Do We Live This Life Intelligently?

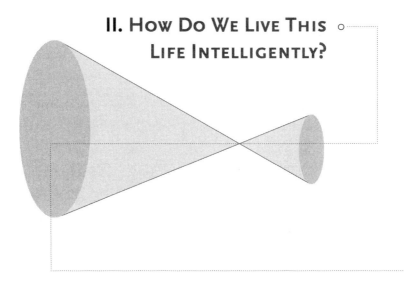

7

LIFE IS RELATIONSHIP WITH OTHERS

WHAT IS LIFE? Here, I will define life as an existence wherein self and other are divided and opposed to one another.

Paramecia seem not to have, as we humans have, an awareness of opposition between self and other. But perhaps when a paramecium approaches nearby food to absorb it into its body, the simple mechanical act of encountering and taking in something that was outside of itself presents a very subtle, basic sense of distinction. Similarly, perhaps when trees dry up and wither due to lack of water and pollution, they experience the world of opposition between self and other. Animals seem to have some awareness of the opposition of self and other: a bird, for instance, will fight fiercely to expel an intruder that enters into its territory. Continuing on up the chain of evolution in this manner, we find that human beings experience the highest degree of opposition between self and other.

This awareness of opposition shapes our personal lives in the form of love and hate between parents and children, in-laws, or friends and strangers. It takes the form of jealousy and competition in the workplace. It provokes clashes over profit and ideology between nations and peoples on a grand scale. Among its greatest products is war—the greatest and most foolish act that human beings can commit.

I once visited the Great Wall of China. Most of the tourists there were excited at the sight of this majestic structure; I decided not to visit it a second time. The Wall made me think of all the infamously foolish deeds committed by humankind down through history. That great wall, which stretches thousands of kilometers, is a wonderful product of history. But how brutal must the emperor and the ministers have been in building it! The multitude of laborers who began the construction work made up one third of the population at the time of the first emperor. The number of people who died carrying out this severe labor is estimated to have been in the hundreds of thousands. How terrible!

The Great Wall, constructed to bar invaders, also made me think about our long human history of war. War isn't just something that happened in the past. Even today, there is almost no corner on Earth untouched by war. It seems as if this stupid behavior will persist as long as humankind persists. But should we be fatalistically resigned to it? Is there no way to control it?

As we have already established, the moment that we begin to think of "I" and "mine," we imagine that "I" and "mine" really exist. The fact that our use of the words and concepts for "I" and "mine" create a false impression is not the only problem. On top of this misperception, we grow attached to a ghost-like self because of these notions. The importance that we place on ourselves leads to fierce rivalries with others, whom we also mistakenly believe to really exist. This leads to nothing but suffering and worry.

Worry and suffering bleed from individuals into society, the nation, and the universe. Looking at the state of a country like Japan, we see that because of the worry and suffering caused by distinctions between self and other, Japan is a ship destined to sink. Our society is beset with murders, bullying in middle school, corruption at the top of the economic world, factional disputes among politicians, the constant splitting of religion into new sects, and so on and so forth. Pick up any newspaper and you find only sorrowful news. If I reflect on these problems, I can only feel that we Japanese are wandering through a very long dark tunnel.

But it isn't only Japan that suffers this calamity; the continued existence of life on Earth is threatened by the destruction of the environment and global warming owing to the excessive discharge of carbon dioxide. I may be a bit melodramatic, but I don't think I am the only one who feels that humanity is plunging toward the dreadful bottom hell. Do we have the means to save our society and humanity that has lost its direction under the heavy burden of suffering? There is no other way than to fundamentally reform our way of knowing the world. We must free ourselves from ways of life founded on egoism, on the opposition of self and other. In other words, there is no other way than to transcend what it means to be a human being, while maintaining our humanity. It is a task akin to restoring the pyramid by righting each stone.

The wish to make ourselves better, to transform ourselves, is a wish that embraces all people. So how do we do it? From the perspective of Representation Only, self-transformation is accomplished by hearing the true teaching, and by cultivating nonconceptual wisdom (*nirvikalpa-jñāna*).

Let's begin with hearing the true teaching. I have already established that human beings are bewildered by words, mistaking them for what they denote, and hence incur suffering. Since we are led astray by language, we must first and foremost extricate ourselves from the illusion of realness that uncritical use of language brings about. When we hear the true teachings of the Buddha, we begin to reflect on the reality that words present and to investigate their veracity. The ideas contained within the true teachings, when reflected upon, begin to nourish pure seeds, latent deep within the store consciousness. As these seeds begin to flourish and grow, our perspective on the world changes. So we must seek out, as much as possible, the true teaching from true teachers, and listen to them often.

But where do we start? What are the basic teachings that we should hear, trust in, and take as a guide for our lives? I myself found the idea of "the way of the bodhisattva" deeply inspiring and motivational at the beginning. A bodhisattva is a person filled with great mercy who lives with the vow that he or she shall remain in the world, subject to repeated birth and death, for the benefit of others. When I take this idea to heart, the courage to live gushes forth from within me, and my dread of death seems to vanish. This happens because a pure altruistic wish germi-

○ ···

nates pure seeds in the depths of the store consciousness. This simple example may not completely fulfill the goal of hearing the true teaching, but it is certainly a step in that direction. We are all aware that there are ideas that when heard only once remain deeply impressed in the mind, influencing the flow of our lives. Hearing true teachings operates on the same principle.

When I was in primary school I lived in front of a Zen temple. I used to visit and play with the monks at the temple. It was just after World War II, so their ranks had dwindled, and the religious training may not have been all that rigorous. Still, sometimes I would catch a glimpse of the monks in the Zen hall in meditation during periods of intensive retreat. One day I asked the head monk, "Why do they silently sit like that?" Rather than answering directly, he said, "When I next sit in my room, open the sliding door and look. You will find a pine tree planted right in the middle of the room." My childish mind simply thought, "What nonsense!" Nevertheless, I came away with the impression that meditation was something wonderful. The head monk's words lingered deep in my mind, leaving a powerful impression. In truth, that statement may have been the reason for my abiding interest in Buddhism.

Another way of taking advantage of this principle is to make a habit of truly rejoicing when something wonderful happens. Learn to express your joy. When you eat something delicious, say, "How delicious!" When you see a beautiful flower, admiringly say, "How beautiful!" When you meet with things that are pleasant, be happy. When we learn to recognize and express positive things in life, the mind becomes positive too. We become happy, elated, and beautiful. The thoughts in our minds and the words that we speak become conditions that germinate positive seeds in the store consciousness. Learning to appreciate beauty and goodness can transform our minds into something beautiful and good.

Similarly, if we always ruminate on the past, thinking "Why did it have to happen like that?" we end up feeling sorry, worrying about things, blaming others, and getting angry. The more negative are our thoughts, the more they contaminate the mind. The fact is that the past has already come and gone, and no matter how much we grumble, we can't change it. It is better to force ourselves out of such types of negative thinking, to remember any of the enjoyable or wonderful things we have experienced, and think instead, "Ah! How enjoyable it was! How wonderful it was!" By doing so, rather than allowing the past to drag us down in the present, we can use it to enliven us in the present. Positive thoughts cultivate pure seeds deep within the store consciousness, and make the mind peaceful and happy.

Now let's turn to the second means of self-transformation: nonconceptual wisdom. When I give something to someone, I serve as the giver of that thing, while the other person becomes the receiver; in between us is the thing given. These three categories structure my basic experience of the act. Although it happens without my being much aware of it, a bit of pride from giving wells up in me. It would be a lie to say I didn't feel this pride. This is a frustrating situation. By giving to another—an act designed to benefit another—ego consciousness may paradoxically grow stronger. We shouldn't give in this way. It is important that we do not allow the conceptual distinctions between giver, receiver, and the thing given to taint our act of giving. Taking action without clinging to the concepts of agent, patient, and object is to act with nonconceptual wisdom.

Nonconceptual wisdom operates in two ways: on one hand it produces a true and pure action for the sake of others, and on the other it is like a fire that turns in on oneself to burn away contaminated seeds in the store consciousness. Just as when a candle burns it emits light and heat and also exhausts its fuel, likewise, nonconceptual wisdom produces compassionate actions for others while consuming the fuel of the passions.

When I was in my early twenties, I was on the verge of becoming a monk. I hoped to live a wonderful life of serenity by diving headfirst into the "Way of Zen." Those days, when I came home from classes at the university, I would go directly to my room, burn a stick of incense, and sit in meditation. Whenever my mother and younger brother watched television, I would lecture them about how bad it was for human beings to waste time, because we had to work diligently until our deaths. I was burning with the motivation to save all people, which I thought I would do by running away to a Zen temple in the mountains and attaining enlightenment there. I'm not saying that I was completely wrong in my thinking then, but when I look at the situation now, I feel sure that it would be nearly impossible to save anyone by doing that. If I cannot act with nonconceptual wisdom, then whether I am a monk or a layperson, my Buddhist practice will not be authentic. Representation Only philosophy particularly emphasizes this point.

How do we rid ourselves of ego consciousness? Merely reading books or hearing teachings from other people will not remove ego consciousness. Deep self-transformation is only possible when we engage in actions that have the power to melt away the ego. In order to have a true practice, we must not only found actions such as giving on nonconceptual wisdom, but must be able to perform any action at all—cleaning, washing, cooking, and so on—with nonconceptual wisdom. It is only through continuous cultivation of nonconceptual wisdom that we will be able to burn away negative seeds in the store consciousness and bring positive qualities to fruition.

We must work among others without discrimination. Working in this way, the corrupt seeds that the ego has planted in the store consciousness will be burned away, and as a result, the smell of the ego will fade, little by little, from our thoughts and actions. This is a truly wonderful practice.

8

THE THEORY OF INTERDEPENDENCY

THESE DAYS, if I find a seat in the train, I think that it would be a fitting thing to say a heartfelt thanks to the person standing in front of me. Ordinarily, of course, we wouldn't think about it. We feel, even if we do not say so, that it is only natural that we should be sitting down after waiting for the train, boarding, and finding a seat.

Let's think a bit more deeply about it. It is only because that person is standing that it's possible for me to sit. This is a fact. To be sure, it is also a fact that I boarded the train earlier, and by the time he boarded there were no more vacant seats. Both the former and the latter are facts. In this way, depending on how we see the state of affairs, according to differences in perspective, the "facts" may differ.

Why do the facts differ between these two perspectives? First of all, I thought it natural to sit, because I did not think about the relationship between myself and the person standing before me. I merely sat, thinking to myself, "Ah! I got a seat." Even if only on a subconscious level, I am automatically assuming that self is self and other is other and that both are distinct substances. The ego consciousness is at work in all such subtle thoughts. But if I train myself to recognize that self and other actually exist in relationship with one another, then I feel an impulse to express thanks whenever I sit—I realize that it is only because of another's standing that I am able to sit.

But we often fail to view things like that, because our minds are contaminated with ego consciousness. If, on the other hand, we look at things from a perspective untainted by ego consciousness, another world becomes visible. We become aware of the truth that we exist by the grace of the existence of others. Buddhists refer to this way of thinking as the theory of interdependency, expressed formulaically as "When this exists, so too does that; when that ceases to be, so too does this."

This theory of interdependency reflects the fundamental principle that underlies all other laws, whether physical, psychological, or ethical. Ethics, for example, teaches that human beings should love, respect, and be grateful to one another. Our philosophies and beliefs grow in complexity when we try to justify acting otherwise. But when we quietly consider the simple fact of interdependency, feelings of thanks and respect for others naturally well up. The next time that I get a seat in a crowded train, I should express thanks, even if only silently in my mind, to the person standing in front of me, because I am only privileged to sit by virtue of keeping them standing. This is a fact. In this way, when we grasp things in a relational way in accordance with the theory of interdependency, it becomes possible to recognize fact as fact, rather than holding conflicting perspectives based on the distinction between self and other.

○ ···

We typically understand things with discrimination that differentiates between self and other—the self is the self, and the other is the other. We easily settle into the open seat. However, if we think of things from the perspective of interdependent relationship, we naturally develop an ethical viewpoint, whether or not we have faith. When we approach life with this perspective it becomes much easier to live among people with a greater degree of gentleness and freedom than we typically have.

Normally when we ride the train we are lost in our own heads, oblivious to one another. We don't want to be bothered; we think we have the right to be alone with ourselves. This is due to habitually assuming that we exist apart from others—that we exist in isolation. But when we look more deeply into things, we see that such a solitary self does not exist. I am not sitting alone on a seat in the train; I am mingling with the people who sit facing me on the other side. These other people reflect me and each other. If there are ten people in the car, I appear in the minds of each of them as an image. I want to cry out to each of them, "You are not sitting alone! You are reflected in each of the people sitting in front of you!"

My life is transformed when I am aware of the fact that I am manifested in the minds of others—when I am aware that we all overflow into one another. I will be naturally inclined to give way to the other if I collide with him or her while walking along the sidewalk, or to hold the door open for others if I reach the entrance to the building first. These are very simple changes, but they profoundly affect how we see ourselves in the world. As our actions change, the feeling of living in harmony with others naturally wells up in the manifold activities of our daily lives.

People exist interdependently. I learned something about this through the practice of martial arts. Japanese martial arts use a concept called *aiki*, which means "aligning power." The idea is that when two fighters clasp hands, if one pushes with a force of twenty pounds, the other must withdraw with equal force in order to escape. If one fighter withdraws with a force of twenty pounds, the other must pursue with the same power. When fighters employ this principle, the hands of both fighters remain inseparably connected, and they have a sense of the tension and movement in each other's bodies. This is the general theory of jūjutsu: pull when pushed; push when pulled. We can apply this principle to our lives, as well, as it is in harmony with the notion of interdependence.

Aside from learning to respond appropriately to others, how should we approach others with our actions in the first place? One of the first practices that Buddhists undertake in order to cultivate themselves is the practice of giving. If we are not wealthy or if we feel particularly attached to whatever we have, we can begin our practice of giving in the simplest way. I don't remember exactly when I learned that I could give, even when I had no money, but I do remember how relaxed it made me feel when it comes to giving. There is something reassuring in the notion that we will still be able to do some good for others even when we are old and infirm. How is it possible?

Always approach others with a gentle face and lovely, graceful words. If we could attain this, how fantastic it would be! A gentle face and lovely words are truly important, especially when we grow old, physically weak, and find it more difficult to do things for others. But a gentle face and loving words always bring happiness and a feeling of relief to others. Even if you have no money, you can give this gift to others.

In general we fear getting older and look at it negatively. It's true that there are certain detrimental aspects of aging, but its positive aspects are greater. For example, we carry the full weight of the long lifetime of experience that we have accumulated until that point. Having long experience shouldn't be a bad thing for others or for yourself. Just as green fruit matures and ripens to attain a flavorful mellowness, so too do we humans mature and ripen, developing a state of mind that is beautiful and bears refined tastes. As I advance in age, I hope to become the sort of person who causes warm feelings to arise in other people, even when sitting silently on the train.

We obtain the energy to live by eating food. Given the role that eating food has in sustaining our very lives, it seems inappropriate to treat the intake of food as a merely mechanical or utilitarian process. Eating food is a splendid opportunity to think about who we are. The simple act of consuming a meal offers us a chance to turn our awareness to a profound truth: our lives are sustained due to the kindness of others.

Try this the next time you eat: first, hold some food in your mouth and focus your awareness on that food. Become one with the taste, slowly and deeply relishing it. If the food is tasty, all the better. When we do this, we automatically become incapable of complaining about our food and a feeling of gratitude will arise.

In order for one person to taste a choice piece of sushi, an infinite number of conditions must be at work: there is the chef who prepared the slice of raw fish; the fisherman who caught the fish; the tuna fish itself; the sea that nurtured it; the first drops of life as they came into being; the world as it was formed with the appropriate balance of elements to support life; the birth of our sun and solar system; the explosion into existence of our universe billions of years ago; and on and on. The chain of causes and effects goes back without end. If any piece of the vast and infinite web of causality has been absent, this particular moment of tasting tuna fish would not have occurred.

Further, let's examine our own bodies. There is the tongue, the nervous system, the brain, and sixty billions or so cells, all cooperatively working to enable us to relish the taste of our food. We can also see the chain of causes and effects that formed this body: from primordial life to our simian ancestors; from our parents' sperm and ovum to our birth; through our early environment and our education. There are also those things that support our present self in the space it immediately occupies: the earth on which we stand, the world that holds this body against it with the force of gravity, and the sun that gives it light and warmth; further away are the distant stars. All of these support us, too. It makes no difference whether they are close at hand or at the furthest reaches of the universe.

The fact is that we live and are supported by an infinite number of powers other than ourselves. Even this is not entirely accurate. I speak of "other powers beside ourselves," but ultimately there are only these "other powers." The impression of "ourselves" is simply imagined and projected onto the confluence of causal and conditioning factors. As our wisdom grows this imagined self at the center of things will shrink, bit by bit, until finally it disappears.

Returning to the example of tasting food, into my mouth goes the sliced raw fish. Of course, I typically think to myself, "I love the taste of fish!" But "I" am not tasting it. Taste would not happen without a tongue, nerves, and a brain. My taste buds and other senses all contribute to the experience of taste. Tasting delicious fish, I feel happy. The happiness that I feel doesn't just come from the fish, or from myself. And it doesn't just pop out of nowhere. The simple experience of tasting something delicious is wholly supported by other powers, by innumerable and infinite relations. Knowing this, I am filled with a feeling of gratitude. Thank you tongue! Thank you brain! Thank you sliced fish, fisherman, sun, and earth!

With wisdom like this we can begin to live each day with gratitude. The spread of this sort of attitude becomes the basis for a human society in which we are grateful to others and care for them.

Here, too, we see yet another argument for the non-existence of the "self"—namely, it only exists based on immeasurable and innumerable conditions other than itself. This is another key point of Buddhist philosophy: everything lacks a "self" because

everything is interdependent. This idea holds within it the medicine that extinguishes obstinate ego consciousness. Realizing
that the "self" only exists as the collocation of an infinite number
of conditions, and is nothing more than this, I grow suspicious
of the conviction with which I feel "I am." The thought that this
"me" is only an echo of the notion of "me," and that what this
notion points to does not actually exist, begins to really hit home.

So, we can see that the destruction of ego consciousness is tied
up with our development of a sense of gratitude toward others.
As we contemplate the web of interdependence, we simultaneously grow more responsive to and integrated with others and
less involved with the self-centered work of ego consciousness.

I once went on a one-day tour of Nara that the student activity
department of my university sponsored. We all stayed overnight
at a temple in Nara. It was the first experience of staying in a
temple for the majority of the students, and each of them seems
to really have found it memorable. But they all shared in common one painful experience: squatting to eat breakfast. At breakfast all of the students squatted together with several monks and
ate without a word. As breakfast wore on, their squatting legs
became numb and painful, and I noticed a large number of students impatiently changing the positions of both legs, sheep-
ishly grinning as they did so. In contemporary Japan, almost no
one squats for long periods anymore, so these kids were totally
unprepared for half an hour of squatting.

Ordinarily when we look at our legs, we think, "Ah, *my* legs."
These legs belong to us and we think that we can move them

freely, however we wish. But when our legs grow painful from squatting for a long time, we suddenly find that these legs, which we thought of as our property, don't function as we want them to. And when our legs fall asleep, we definitely get the sense that they are not "ours," but something we depend upon. Even temporarily losing the ability to use our legs brings home the thought that we depend on our legs to live. We come to realize how grateful we should be for the existence of our legs, and all the other parts of our bodies.

When I began my studies in Buddhism, I was astounded and excited when I encountered a pair of concepts in a list of the various types of causal conditions: efficacious governing conditions and inefficacious governing conditions. Governing conditions that are efficacious positively contribute to the emergence of things, exerting some power that brings those things into being. It could be the sun in relation to plants that grow, or in the case of people, parents who give birth to us and the friends and family who extend a helping hand in times of difficulty. Inefficacious governing conditions, also called "governing conditions that do not impinge," are those conditions that make the existence of a thing possible without directly contributing to it. This refers to things like the roof over my head, which doesn't directly contribute to my existence but does so indirectly by protecting me from the elements.

This idea really opened my mind. Of course, we all know that without our parents or friends, without food, water, and air, we would have quite a hard time staying alive. But when I expanded my thought to include those things that only indirectly contributed to my existence, from anonymous people with whom I ride the train to mundane objects like furniture and dishware, an indescribable feeling of gratitude began to well up inside my heart. The idea that I had clung to as "me" or my "self" shriveled up into a tiny, inconsequential thing. It was as if my life was born anew, filled with boundless potential.

9.

Love Comes from the Source

Owing to the eye-opening advance of the natural sciences, we have come to know that the life on earth began almost 36 billion years ago. We know of no other life in our solar system except for what we find here on Earth. Voyager 1, a space research satellite launched in 1977 to study the solar system has already passed Neptune and the solar system, without discovering signs of life. We may never discover another star system with a satellite like the earth, teeming with life. The world is truly a rare heavenly body that abounds with the power of life!

I once had the opportunity to spend a week during the summer at a friend's villa at Tadeshina. Breathing in the fresh morning air, I would enjoy strolling through the forest and valley. What beautiful high-altitude plants I encountered while walking! I learned their names from my friend and marveled at the beautiful creations of nature, their naturally woven shapes, rich in colors and patterns. The vitality of nature is truly wondrous. I once saw a photo in the newspaper, taken by a submarine from the marine research center at a depth of 6,500 meters below the surface, that showed a sea slug living in the pitch black depths.

How surprising to learn that there are substantial living creatures at such depths, living on microscopic plankton!

How have the innumerable varieties of living beings come to exist on this earth? One possible answer to this question is, of course, that a divine creator made them according to some sort of cosmic plan. As you have probably already guessed, I don't believe this. As I tend more towards science and philosophy in my thought, I like to think that there is some sort of universal life power that all living things share in common, and that the various forms of life emerge based on the ongoing expression of this basic biological element. I presume that all living things, even trees and plants, bacteria and tiny insects, possess the will to live—all life wants to live. Owing to this basic will to live, bacteria repeat cell division and insects reproduce to ensure the survival of their species.

I also presume that self-attachment lies behind the basic will to live. You may object that since plants do not have minds, there is no way that they could have the mental state of attachment. But the mind of attachment that I speak of need not necessarily be like the mental states found in human beings, which are strongly tangled up with words and feelings. What I want to say is that the very state of being alive already includes, in some subtle sense, the activity of self-attachment, even if it is expressed much more subtly than it is in humans. The mind in the "mind of attachment" may be expressed simply as a self-protective, self-propagating energy, which, although extremely subtle, exists within all life.

○ ···

The universal life-power that I have proposed above is just this activity or energy. It is the life concealed within each bacterium, each insect, each animal, and each of us human beings. For the time being I'd like to call this universal power "the source" of life. I call it this because this power of life is like the root that is the source from which shoots sprout forth to become a trunk, and from which the trunk divides, spreading out into numerous braches, and from which each branch divides, spreading a beautiful canopy of wonderfully variegated leaves. In this metaphor each of those leaves represents an individual living being. Though we differ in size and shape, all of us living beings share a common source: the desire to live.

From here I would like to jump to the idea that to truly love another is to recognize that shared source within them, and to love them from there. This idea brings to my mind the words of my favorite saint, Yājñavalkya:

> A husband does not become lovable by being loved;
> the husband becomes lovable by loving *ātman*.
> The wife does not become lovable by being loved;
> it is by loving *ātman* that she becomes lovable.

Ātman in these lines refers to the true reality of each individual, which is at the same time the universal true reality that transcends each individual. Yājñavalkya is saying that to love another is not merely to love them as an individual, but to love the universal true reality within them. Admittedly, my idea of the source has been influenced by Yājñavalkya's lovely sentiment about ātman here. I am convinced that loving another means to love the source, the basic vital activity within them.

However, it is often difficult to maintain this sense of love. A very strong sense of self-attachment is at work within me, and the ego consciousness actively colors whatever I experience. As a result I sometimes end up perceiving others as "my" others. If we aren't careful, ego consciousness can distort our perceptions of even something as pure as the source of life that we all share in common. An extreme example of this type of selfish love is when a parent who wants to commit suicide kills their child first. We see stories like this in the news from time to time. This is a truly foolish act that makes me angry. From my point of view, it indicates that the parent has become incapable of recognizing the source, the wish to live, within their child. Children are certainly born from the source that we all share, yet these parents drag them along to death, based on the strength of the distorted view that they are "*my* children." This is an extreme example, but the same distortion is at work in many relationships where love becomes something based on the other being "my boyfriend," "my girlfriend," "my husband," or "my wife."

So it is extremely important that we destroy the ego consciousness—not only to ensure our own happiness, but also so that we may truly love others. This is even more true in the twenty-first century, when our expanding global population and dwindling resources leave little room for selfish behavior. We must shoulder the burden of managing our world together. Let's bring an end to dualistic thought!

"Dualistic thought" refers to seeing the world in terms of dual opposites. This way of thinking divides everything into "this" and "not this." Some of our most basic conceptual categories are formed in this manner: "is" and "is not," "self" and "other," "one" and "many," "good" and "bad," and so on. This way of thinking by contradistinction rests at the heart of our common social, economic, and political life. But placing too much stock in these dialectic categories leads to many problems. Most fundamentally, we begin to think that these categories exist the way they are perceived, independent of language and concepts. Opposition is projected onto the world around us until it completely surrounds and swallows us.

Dualistic categories are so basic to our thought that it can be hard to challenge them. But we must honestly ask ourselves: are self and other really different in reality? Do the concepts "is" and "is not" really capture the way things are? When we toss the concepts "is" and "is not" out while reflecting deeply on the nature of reality, they suddenly disappear like drops of water thrown onto a hot frying pan.

There are countless religions crisscrossing the globe and frequently coming into contact with one another. From religion to religion beliefs may differ regarding the soul, the afterlife, sin, and redemption. But I think that all religions can basically agree that things do not really exist the way that they appear. From my perspective, this is something that all humans accept and is the basis on which all religions can coexist. That we intuitively know this explains why we have so much admiration for those who are not enticed by the superficial pleasures of the world.

When we ourselves begin to grow convinced that things do not really exist the way that they appear, the world begins to appear to us in a more immediate, possibility-filled way, where "is not" means just about as much as "is." While under the influence of dualistic thought, we desperately cling to existence and desperately fear non-existence. We now exist, but we are afraid of death because it brings our existence to an end. As the grip of dualistic thought loosens, that fear begins to fade.

It is true that our view of things is not easy to change. But trust that if you reflect on these matters, a new life will appear!

But this is all rather abstract. How are we to make use of this view in our daily lives? Take our sense of "self": it is precisely because I unquestioningly accept the idea that there is a "self," an "I," who lives through and experiences this life that suffering and worry arise. We compare ourselves with others and feel that we are inferior. We ask, "Why am I like this?" We worry that this or that person hates me. We fear that those who love us will leave. There is really no end to the anxiety that comes with clinging to ourselves. By the same token, we break down and cry when we think that this "self" will someday cease to exist. Tossed between the extremes of being and nonbeing, we find no peace.

When people first hear that there is no self, the impulse is often to swing to the opposite end of the spectrum: absolute nonexistence. But we ourselves, our lives, are not an absolute nonexistence. We don't exist in the over-exaggerated way that our minds tend to think we do, but neither are we absolutely nonexistent. It would be ideal if we could immediately be aware of this fact, rather than rectifying our thinking bit by bit. But it takes time to change our habits. And even when we have let go of this idea of "self," we still have to take care of ourselves and we have a responsibility to others. Neither self nor other exist as they appear to. It is their deep interdependence that makes them this way. Keep this in mind as you work on letting go of self-involvement.

I presume, given the abysmal state of what appears in the news each day, that I am not the only one who loathes to read the newspaper anymore. Why do the kinds of catastrophes reported there happen in this world? I think the fundamental cause lies in the fact that we allow ourselves to be deluded by what our own minds project onto the world, thinking that chasing after what we imagine to be satisfying will make us happy.

The spectacle available to our present age emphatically does not entice us to transform our way of life by seeking happiness within ourselves rather than in money, grades, or fame. So it is up to us to turn our minds inward to investigate the Big Bang that our minds create. It is generally accepted that the universe came into being with the Big Bang approximately 150 billion years ago, and that even now the universe continues to expand. This is true so far as contemporary science is concerned, but it is an abstract fact for us, rather than a directly experienced fact. But we know directly the Big Bang that our minds create each morning. We can say that every morning begins with a "Big Bang." The moment we arise from the depths of sleep, beyond space and time, the whole boundless world, established in time and space, manifests to us in a single stroke. This is a tangible fact that we can experience every morning.

The world, fashioned in this way by a "Big Bang," is immediately transfigured into a world of separated existences, of "selves" and "others." There come up thoughts like, "What do I have to do today?" "Today I have to accomplish such and such, even though I don't want to." In this way, as soon as we awake, the "raw world" is complexly colored with words and thoughts, these feelings of worry; it is transformed into a world of dualism. I live each day within this world exploded from the daily Big Bang of my mind, oscillating right and left.

We must cultivate a mind not so easily influenced by words, thoughts, and feelings. Buffeted by words and thoughts, we have lost sight of the true way of life. I think to myself, "That person is hateful!" and then I speak to them as if that's how they are. But if the notion of hate had not appeared in my mind, no such hateful person would appear before me. A person as such is neither hateful nor non-hateful. I color the person as hateful with thoughts and words. This is how the world we perceive has already become other than it truly is. I produced it, so it may be better to say that I have caused it to appear other than it is.

The world outside of ourselves remains a world without names, uncolored by our emotions. The world was like that the moment we woke from sleep. But our minds automatically transformed it into a world where the self and the other are opposed, where thinking and worry about many things constantly bubbles up, even leading to anger and fights. Thus each day comes into being and comes to an end. Months and years pass, and this life of hate, fight, and worry passes away as if in an instant. What vanity this life is! We must decide to get out of this morass as quickly as we can.

What is the best way to get out of it? First we must develop the power to return to the true world, without names and uncolored by emotion, from the world of confusions and dualistic thought. We must practice meditation so that the workings of the mind give way to mindfulness, concentration, and wisdom. "Mindfulness" is the capacity to "mark clearly and not forget." It refers to the power to preserve an image in the mind, to remember it clearly, and to always be capable of recollecting it without losing it. When we practice meditation and concentrate steadily on the breath until we feel unsure whether it is we who are breathing or the breathing that is us, dualistic opposition vanishes and the quiet, settled mind appears. This is what is meant by "concentration." The world "as it is" comes to the surface in this settled mind, stripped of all thought and emotion. This is the working of "wisdom."

In this way, a mind that starts from mindfulness develops into concentration and wisdom. By repeatedly refining this process, we ourselves will be able to obtain something wonderful in the mind, something that we were not aware of until now. Money, rank, fame, and the like are things acquired from the outside world. They are really good for nothing in the long run. How much more important it is to realize that what is most important exists in the depths of our own minds and cannot be taken away from us!

10

Forgetting the Self

We necessarily assume some kind of substantial thing whenever we use words to denote forms. If we use the word I then we presuppose that something called "I" exists. By speaking in this way, we make an imagined thing, something that doesn't really exist, into something strong and weighty; we inflate its pseudo-reality.

This kind of inflation of imagined realities leads to all sorts of problems and conflict, from household disputes between mothers-in-law and daughters-in-law all the way up to international conflict. The fact is that we must forget ourselves, our families, our nations, and our religious sectarianism. None of these imagined enemies or sources of dispute even really exist. What exists is only the activity of the mind and the development of its energy.

In fact, everything is only a transformation of energy, and all actions are transitory. Everything that is made, composed, or comes into being depending on causes and conditions is impermanent. The self is projected onto a continuum of fleeting mental and physical aggregates that arise and perish in each moment. To arrest this flow of energy and try to enclose it within the notion of "self" is a mistake. But can we understand what this "self" really is without relying on words and thought?

Once, an artist friend of mine from Switzerland proposed that we spend some time living together on a solitary island, where we would refrain from using words as much as we possibly could. The idea was that this might help us to come to know each other more intimately. It is certainly an interesting thought. If we were truly able to speak in a way that leaves behind any reference to "I," we certainly would experience a new human relationship, one of non-opposition.

It is very difficult for human beings to put an end to the ego. To empty oneself and work for the other is easier said than done. We human beings are centered on ourselves, and it is no exaggeration to say that we live for ourselves. When walking along the sidewalk, I expect others to give way. When I enter the train I expect a seat. It seems impossible that regular people like us will do anything that doesn't turn to our own benefit. If we are totally honest with ourselves, even the good things we do make us feel good, and so benefit us. This isn't just a question of actions, either. With respect to our personal judgments we place ourselves at the center, too. When we disagree with someone, we are quick to judge them harshly and content to label them along a single dimension: "He's so hateful!"

So, how do we put an end to this? No solution short of the total removal of self-centered judgments and actions goes far enough. Ultimately, we must abandon ego consciousness—the cause that lies at the root of all these types of selfish actions and judgments. When it comes down to it, there is nothing for it but to completely forget ourselves.

Still, to lose one's ego is difficult. It is all well and good to think about doing it in our heads, but deep inside we won't hear of it. But there is a method. It is called "seeing by becoming one with the other." The first step is to become aware of the source of our perceptions of others. We see someone we hate and think, "He's so hateful" or "Here comes that detestable jerk." Taking a step back to quietly analyze the mind, we become aware that we only see a hateful person because the feeling of hate has arisen in our own minds. When the feeling of hate doesn't arise, we don't see a hateful person. This is the reality.

Then, being aware of this fact, we must decide to become one with the hateful person; we must put ourselves in his or her shoes. When the thought of hate vanishes I become aware of other aspects of the person, aspects that I was not aware of until now. Slowly I begin to see a richer picture of who this person is, aside from my own feelings about them. Of course, doing this experiment just once will not remove the feeling of hate altogether. We must make a repeated effort, reminding ourselves that hating another person torments both us and them.

We must extend our practice of becoming one with others to listening as well. It is important to really hear what others have to say, and we can do so by again placing ourselves in their shoes. It is useless, as so often happens, to argue while sticking only to one's own standpoint. If we do this, how will we ever develop a meaningful and significant discussion? So we must try to maintain an attitude of listening to others from their own perspectives.

Giving up the attitude that says, "I'm right, and you're wrong," we must work as much as we can to bridge the distance between us. When we listen and relate to others in a genuine way, making an effort to become one with them, their words have the ability to penetrate into the deepest layers of our minds, and we begin to see them more clearly, as they really are. Consequently, a region of our own mind about which we never even think begins to vibrate with the words of the other; back out on the surface of our mind a new voice of the other emerges, one that is different from the one we heard until then. This leads to a new dawn in the relationship between ourselves and those we interact with.

In India, the concept of *samsara* ("circling") is used to convey the idea of endless wandering in the cycle of birth and death. The basic doctrine, common to many religious traditions, is that we endlessly drift in the great sea of suffering, where we are born and die many times. If we perform some bad deed in this life, we will go to hell or some other miserable destiny in the next; on the other hand if we perform some good deed, we will go to heaven. Samsara extends from the past to the present and from the present to the future. As a matter of faith, this concept becomes the foundation for an entire ethical approach to life.

We can also think of transmigration as something that happens within the boundaries of our present lives. For example, my everyday life is like a circle drawn over and over on a piece of paper. We could consider this to be samsara, too. There is little

○ ··

change or development in this flat, circular motion, always rotating around the same place. My everyday life is a life of inertia, without an aim, a life of no change in mental state or environment, day after day, year after year. It is a life lived in gossip and relaxation. To exaggerate a bit it is a bit like hell!

What power is there that can transform this two-dimensional circular motion into a three-dimensional upward spiral? It is an altruistic will—a will that strives to live toward an altruistic aim. And what is this altruistic aim? What is this altruistic will? An altruistic aim is an aim that reaches beyond the individual to embrace all life in common. Given that we are "a single person, a single world," the actions that we perform, tainted by the obstinate ego consciousness, constantly turn back their focus onto ourselves, rather than on others. When I think that I have done something good for others, in silent, honest self-reflection I find that I have done it mainly for myself. Each day's actions return to myself, and I grow heavier and heavier, pressed into the wandering circle of my self-centered life. It grows more and more difficult to push the trajectory of this cycle upwards into a spiral movement. You can see how crucial it is to cast about for an altruistic aim, and to activate the altruistic will to accomplish it.

The weight of our ego consciousness, the drag of our attachment and self-love, keeps us from discovering the joy of doing something genuine for others. We must scrape off this crusty, barnacled ego consciousness, little by little. Then the altruistic aim begins to appear, little by little.

It takes resolve to accomplish this. First, resolve to reduce your ego. Make a vow, or at least think to yourself with conviction: "Not for myself, but for the world, for other beings, I shall continue to burn the energy that I have been given." With progress through diligent effort every day, in no time the ego, left unfed, will begin to dwindle.

It is often very difficult to translate into practice the idea "not for myself." The obstinate ego consciousness, latent in the depths, does not permit it. Even if we have to force ourselves a bit, let's work at saying, "Anything is fine for myself." These words and this thought are slowly imbued into the depths of the mind, where they awaken the altruistic will that resides latently deep within us. It answers the call: "Good! At last I will acquire some wisdom. Let me live for those who are suffering." The desire to seek wisdom and to transmit compassion waxes. By upholding this feeling, we begin to rise from the flat, circular trajectory of our lives into an upward spiral that leads to true life.

Life based on altruistic will, with its great aim, unflinchingly challenges suffering and hardship, does not take pride in favorable circumstances, and is not attached to pleasures. Since this "upward spiral" makes it possible to turn freely in three-dimensional space, instead of tracing the same circuit over and over again, it opens our lives to new experiences. The more people we encounter, the broader the diameter of the spiral becomes. The person who lives this upward spiral is called a *bodhisattva* and lives by two great vows: to seek enlightenment above and to transform sentient beings below.

○ ···

11

THE THREE GREAT AIMS IN LIFE

I HAVE PROPOSED that we lead a life with a great aim founded on altruistic will. What do I mean by "aim?" An aim is the grand goal that we keep in our sights as we work slowly toward it, without being distracted. When climbing a mountain, for example, we aim for the top and keep our eyes on it as we proceed up the trail. If we lose sight of the peak, we may veer off the main trail, get side-tracked, and become lost or even lose our lives. Likewise, as we make our way through this life, a great aim serves to keep us on track. Without a great aim, we may end up side-tracked, mired in a life of illusion.

But what is the great aim of life? You may think that since everyone is different, each must have different goals in life. This is answer is all right, but it must refer to aims other than the great aim. Usually these types of aims turn out to be nothing but a stop along the way. Great aims are those aims that all beings share in. So what are they? There are three:

1. To learn about oneself.
2. To resolve the matter of life and death.
3. To save others.

These three aims are outlined in the famous introductory Zen text, *Ten Ox-Herding Pictures*. *Ten Ox-Herding Pictures* is a text that symbolically depicts the mental attitudes that arise through the practice of Zen as a narrative in ten stages using the characters of an ox and an ox-herder. I shall explain this in a simple way. One day the herder found that one of the bulls had run away from the pen. The herder, Hotei, starts his journey in search of the bull (stage one: "searching for the bull"). After searching for many days, he finds the footprints of the bull (stage two: "seeing the footprints"). Joyfully and courageously following the footprints, he sees the bull at a distance (stage three: "seeing the bull"). Then, coming closer, he catches the bull with the rope he carries (stage four: "catching the bull"). He then tames the wild bull and calms it (stage five: "calming the bull"). Sitting on the back of the calm bull, the herder returns home (stage six: "returning home on the bull"). Once home, he puts the bull in the cattle shed, and sits alone with a peaceful heart (stage seven: "forgetting the bull/the man alone"). The next drawing is the famous subject matter of many ink drawings called "the empty circle," which is indeed the picture of a simple circle (stage eight: "man and bull both forgotten"). This picture symbolizes the state of mind of someone who has attained insight into emptiness, the true reality of himself and all existence. A person thus enlightened has lost his or her ego and is now able to live absolutely naturally (stage nine: "returning to the source"). The next image is of a smiling Hotei entering the marketplace, which represents finally being able to live effectively in the world to save those who are suffering (stage ten: "returning to the marketplace").

These ten pictures help us to understand the three great aims of human life. First, the runaway bull symbolizes our true self. The herder, realizing that he has lost it, sets out in search for it. In other words, he begins looking for his true self. This stage corresponds to the first great aim in human life: learning about oneself. The herder finds the bull, catches it, and henceforth lives his life keeping it close at hand. His mental attitude progresses until he forgets the bull and quietly rests alone. Even if someone told him that he had late-stage cancer, he would remain unperturbed and completely at rest. This is the second great aim in human life, to resolve the matter of life and death. Even so, a lingering attachment to the self yet remains in him. The final shred of ego consciousness is wiped away as he experiences the enlightenment, which we call "the enlightenment that was there all along." This moment is represented pictorially as an empty circle. Finally, as Hotei the herder returns to town, he realizes the final great aim of saving others.

In this way, *Ten Ox-Herding Pictures* superbly and symbolically illustrates the three great aims of life: inquiring into oneself, resolving the problem of life and death, and saving others. Although people differ in terms of beliefs, habits, and thought, these three aims are common to all of humankind.

I am so happy to see that volunteering has become such a normal thing in society. The number of people who substantially give of themselves to others seems to grow yearly. But even with all the physical aid that we give to the ill and dying, I wonder whether it is enough to provide merely physical help to the dying. I wonder whether we should expand our idea of nursing beyond just the treatment of physical, bodily suffering. Perhaps some portion of our efforts should go to helping the ill and dying to resolve the matter of life and death, to be able to find peace despite the fact that life will have to come to an end.

The idea of being a bodhisattva is promising in this regard. The bodhisattva way of life gives us the courage and energy to live. It is a wonderful medicine that removes the fear of death. Although *bodhisattva* is a Buddhist term, the concept itself is something that everyone can relate to—it speaks to our deepest humanity. Bodhisattvas, as people who live by the power of two great vows—to seek enlightenment above and to transform sentient beings below—answer the two most basic questions in life: "What is this life?" and "How should we live it?"

What is this life? As we grow into adulthood we forget this question and lose our sense of curiosity about this life. We get the impression that we already understand everything. But with regard to the basic question of what this life is, we have understood nothing. Where do I come from and where am I going? It seems as if we ourselves only exist in the present moment. Is it even possible for us to comprehend ourselves in this fleeting present moment? A finger cannot point at itself; a knife cannot cut itself. We cannot step outside our "self" to grasp it. In this sense, we have to admit that we don't really know ourselves. Ultimately we do not know anything. Someone who is truly aware of this fact, who becomes determined to know, and who is diligent in their efforts to know, is a bodhisattva. That firm resolve to learn about ourselves is the vow to seek enlightenment above.

On the other hand, we do understand what it is like to wander, to be alone, and to suffer. So, even if we do find some sort of transcendent relief, we feel compelled to do something to save others who are like us. Understanding how we should live this life, what we should strive to do with the time we are given, is the vow to transform sentient beings below. We vow not to cross over ourselves, but to help others cross over first. It is the thought, "Don't worry about me; I must help those who are suffering first." In Buddhist terms, this vow indicates an intention to traverse the cycle of birth and death in order to save all living beings. Technically speaking, a bodhisattva is someone who lives in a state of existence called "nirvana with no residence." This is the form of nirvana characteristic of the Mahayana, or Great Vehicle, of Buddhism, in which one dwells neither in the world of birth and death nor in nirvana beyond it. The goal of the bodhisattva is a nirvana that transcends both samsara and nirvana. Bodhisattvas incarnate within samsara in order to lead others to nirvana, but they are neither attached to nor bound by either.

The concept of the bodhisattva originally referred solely to Śākyamuni Buddha, before he attained his buddhahood. The Buddha appears as a bodhisattva in the collection of stories about his previous lives called the *Jātaka Tales*. These stories contain the prototype for the notion of "nirvana with no residence." These tales capture the wonderful way of life available to us as human beings, which we tend to lose sight of when absorbed in self-centered thinking. The sūtras say that if we piled up all the bones that we have had within our bodies in our previous lives, they would be higher than Mount Everest and that our blood from those lives would amount to more than all the water in the oceans of the world. It is amazing to think of this human life as being the tip of this mountain of previous lives—it is but one mote of dust among millions.

I used to dismiss the notion of samsara, the cycle of birth and death. I did not believe that a relationship of cause and effect linked death and rebirth, or that the cycle would continue as certainly as a stone dropped from the hand will fall. But now that I am older and thinking seriously about what life remains for me, I feel more compelled than ever to live purposefully, with a great aim, rather than to merely prepare for my inevitable death. My life looks more and more like something to be used purposefully, for the benefit of others. I feel unafraid of sacrificing this life, if need be, in order to save someone in need.

Wisdom and compassion are the two great dignities of humanity. Between them, compassion is the means. We must know the correct means in order to successfully develop and deploy compassion. Wisdom is the light that illuminates the world as it truly is—the world of ultimate truth (*paramārtha-satya*), which cannot be described in language. Compassion is the warmth that penetrates the world as we commonly know it—the world of conventional truth (*saṃvṛti-satya*), which is the purview of thought and language.

○ ··

Since the world of conventional truth is the world of language, words carry power there. The words of a vow, for example, speak to the deepest parts of ourselves and have the power to make us actually listen. Thus, we typically speak the words of the vow in a loud voice: "I, like a bodhisattva, will remain in samsara for as long as it takes, continuing my efforts to save others, no matter what may come." The utterance of vows is an expedient means that nourishes the seeds of compassion dormant in the deepest layers of the mind, causing them to sprout and grow.

I have a very strong conviction in the power of these words. I consistently vow that I will not die but will return again as a bodhisattva for the benefit of others. Even if reincarnation does not happen as we Buddhists believe, the words of this vow have a profound effect on how I live my life. I am determined to know myself, to resolve the great matter of life and death, and to save others. To be a bodhisattva is to be a living embodiment of these three great aims.

12

Developing a Culture of Intelligence

Nowadays we champion the sort of education that furthers our sense of individuality. Individuality is undoubtedly important. Systems that suppress individuality, using outside pressure to produce uniform people, like individuals stamped out of a mold, are rightly reviled. Nevertheless, in addition to helping us find ourselves, education must also prepare us to live with others. The collectivity of humanity, after all, is the very ground in which individuality takes root.

In this sense, individuality is common to all human beings. It reflects our essential collectivity. The development and expansion of authentic individuality becomes possible only by first cultivating the shared ground of our collectivity. To grow crops like rice, beans, and tomatoes, for example, we must first till, fertilize, and water the soil in which they are to be grown. If the soil is not properly taken care of, not even the best seed will grow in it.

Human beings are no different. Even if we each have the power to develop our unique individuality, in order to flourish and grow, we rely on those all around us. If we focus only on our own sacred individuality, at the expense of caring about others, we are likely to grow into ill-developed, selfish people. We should all hope to produce a society wherein children are taught to consider others, even as they develop their own unique voices.

Picture an intelligent girl who excels at mathematics and physics. The education she receives brings out her natural intellectual capacity and refines it. When she grows up she uses her intelligence to pursue a career in science. Now, if she had not been taught to cultivate her sense of connectedness to others as well as her sense of individuality, her wonderful talents could well become tools of destruction. This happens all the time in reality and will continue to happen again. Intelligent, well-educated people have created nuclear weapons, toxic pesticides, and methods of torture. Some of the worst war criminals in recent memory have been very well educated.

Twenty-first century humanity is capable of amazing feats. We have decoded the human genome and are learning more and more each day about how to select the traits we'd like our children to have at the genetic level. Sooner or later, we may develop the techniques to create life itself. Living in an era like this, it becomes more necessary than ever that we humans—both those who advance scientific progress and those who enjoy the benefits of such advancement—develop an awareness of the great aims in life and foster it in our societies. We must turn our attention to cultivating our sense of the universal collectivity of human beings.

What is the universal collectivity of human beings? Broadly speaking, we might say it is comprised of the wisdom that under-

○ ···

stands reality and the compassion that enables us to relate to and love others. These two elements exemplify the greatness and dignity of human beings. These two, wisdom and compassion, make an excellent basis for approaching a well-rounded education. We must, of course, cultivate our knowledge about the world and how it works, but we should also devote a good part of our education to considering the way in which who we are and what we do affects others.

The Buddha's final teaching offers us great advice in this respect. As the Buddha was about to die, Ānanda, who had been his closest aid for much of his career, began to cry and worry about what would happen after the Buddha's death. How would the monks live without his support and guidance? To calm his fears, the Buddha said,

> Ānanda, be a light unto yourself. Hold fast to the truth
> as a light.

This line is quite famous. The Buddha constantly taught the doctrine of no-self, but insisted in the end that we must depend on ourselves. The Buddha was an excellent educator. The self that he advises us to rely upon is precisely that self that is "a light" that sees things as they really are. It is also that self that holds to the truth, that holds to the laws of karma and the principle of interdependence. These aspects of ourselves are what bring about wisdom and compassion. A buddha, an awakened being, is one who has fully realized wisdom and compassion. A buddha has perfected the two great dignities of the human being.

At this point, I'd like to return to the two basic questions with which I began this book: "What does it mean to be alive?" and "How should we live?" To sum up everything I've attempted to lay out over the course of this book, it seems safe to say that life is an opportunity, and we should live it in a way that takes full advantage of that opportunity. My goal is to live my life like a lighted candle, using my innate capacities to bring light to others and myself. Once the fuel that sustains this life is burned completely away, I will have to bid farewell. How wonderful it would be if I were able to live like this! The problem, especially for younger generations, is learning how to light the candle. How should we go about helping them learn what they need in order to live a meaningful life?

Until now I have been saying that we human beings must nurture universal togetherness, and that this togetherness consists of wisdom that understands reality and compassion that relates to and loves others. What reality do we need to understand? It is the reality of interdependence and emptiness. We do not exist as independent, substantially existent beings but as deeply interdependent beings that lack any real substance. Life is only possible where there is interdependence. The "self" that we take so seriously and protect even at the cost of harming others is only a concept imputed onto the transient flow of phenomena. A well-rounded education will include reflection on this. As mentioned above, repeatedly reflecting on this concept nourishes the

○ ....

wonderful capacity for wisdom latent deep within the mind and helps it to sprout and grow.

How can we introduce these types of ideas into our education? Here are a few suggestions:

- Because children develop by watching adults whom they respect, teachers—both parents and schoolteachers—must seriously cultivate their own awareness of reality. Before being able to successfully teach children how to live, parents and teachers must educate themselves about it.

- Parents must understand and embody the principle of interdependence. We are not parents by ourselves but only in relation to our children. Of course it is difficult for children to grasp the idea of interdependence, but if parents can model this in their relationship with children at an early age, it makes it easier for them to catch on later.

- Even parents have a hard time restraining themselves when they feel like saying they like or dislike something. In general we feel that freedom means being able to say whatever we want to, but sometimes freedom means being able to exercise restraint. Knowing when to remain silent, particularly when what we want to say is negative, is a useful skill to model.

- Most families share meals together. This makes mealtime a wonderful opportunity to show children how to relate to their experiences. We should learn to focus on and express appreciation for the positive aspects of our food. When it is delicious we should say so. This is also a good time to reflect on the infinite web of causes and effects that produce the meal we are eating. Maintaining a robust sense of wonder regarding simple things like food will reward the child later in life.

- It is also important to learn to concentrate on one thing at a time, taking the time to become one with it. Even young children at play can do this. Many of my clearest memories of childhood in post-war Japan are of playing with other children. We learned to confront our fears and overcome self-doubt by playing together. One kid would jump down from a big pile, and then each of us would challenge ourselves to replicate his feat. When learning to make the jump, my young mind became extremely concentrated. It was frightening, of course, to make the jump, but I learned to confront difficulty and how to make choices by concentrating. Education should teach how to interiorize this power and wield it in actual life situations.

How should we cultivate an intelligent approach to the ideas of *good* and *bad* more generally? Once when I was lecturing I asked my students to spontaneously write down, off the top of their heads, examples of actions or behaviors that are good. Generally, what we ended up with was a list that included things like "helping others," "respecting our parents," "getting good grades," and "doing exercise." When we looked into the various examples we came up with, we found that our shared conception of *good* broke down into four categories:

1. Something that improves a situation
2. Something that benefits health
3. Something that is pleasurable
4. Something skillful, fruitful, or effective

No one would oppose the idea that it is good to help others. But why is it good? We can give many reasons: because they will feel happy, because they will enjoy it, because their suffering will decrease, etc. It is good to help others because it produces happiness, joy, and ease in them. This type of *good* can be called *virtue*. When any of the four types of good are done in relation to others, we can think of them as virtue, because they are not done with any sort of self-centered intention. Generally speaking, actions that lack intention can be neither *virtuous* nor *nonvirtuous*.

On the other hand, sometimes people do things that are good because they feel compelled to. Respecting one's parents, for example, may become merely a duty for many young people. Such actions are technically not *virtuous* because one lacks a true intention when compelled by outside pressure. Respecting our parents becomes a virtue only when we do so out of a genuine sense of gratefulness for all that our parents have done for us.

Inculcating a basic understanding of what it means to be good and how we ought to strive to implement good behavior in our lives will help us to reform our culture so that it becomes a culture of intelligence. We can look to inspiring role models from history for examples of how to cultivate this intelligence throughout one's life.

As a younger man I was fascinated by Katsu Kaishū, the nineteenth-century Japanese statesman famous for handing over Edo Palace without any bloodshed or loss of life by skillfully negotiating with Saigo Takamori. I thought that this man, who survived the confusion of the feudal system, must have been a very clever and wily politician. But when I read *Hikawa Seiwa*, his memoir, I found that Kaishū had purposefully and intelligently forged his character. He writes:

> Thus, for nearly four years I wholeheartedly threw myself into the serious practice of religion. Meditation and fencing became the foundation for my later years. At the hour of the government collapse, when I had crossed into territory where death is certain, I sustained myself thanks to these two things. Even when assassins and other enemies besieged me, I was able to keep my wits and fight them with skill. My courage and spirit were perpetually nourished by those two.

When he was a young man, Kaishū diligently trained in meditation and fencing. He writes that he learned to perfect himself with these practices because he cultivated no-self by means of them.

Whatever you do, you must become no self. The supreme practice that penetrates the Way, that clearly sees into oneself, is nothing other than these two words: no self. You won't necessarily reach this end, no matter how hard you practice meditation. Many are disturbed when things come to a head.

To steel yourself while you are young, as Katsu Kaishū did, is wonderful. It is truly unfortunate that many young people lack any aim in life and are simply swallowed up in the affluence of material things. We must encourage the young to find the will-power to steel themselves as Kaishū was able to do in the face of great difficulty.

Today we place so much emphasis on freedom of choice that it's easy for young people to rationalize quitting or giving up as a "choice," rather than as a failure. What type of "self" does this produce?—one that succumbs too easily to base inclinations, to easiness, and self-indulgence. When young people raised in this way reach a major crossroads in their life, when they encounter a real crisis, it is doubtful whether they will have the power to make a decision and stick to it with conviction.

For Kaishū, meditation and fencing entailed arduous training. But Kaishū had a great aim. He, too, held the vow to live for the world and for others. It is precisely because he observed that vow that he persevered in such strict training even as a young man. The experiences of our youth drastically shape our lives. If you will indulge me, I will relate a bit of my own story here.

When I was young, around twenty years old, I was troubled and suffered from self-consciousness. I decided to pursue meditation at Engakuji in Kamakura, expecting deliverance from my troubles. I stayed for a week at the meditation hall, where ordinary people were allowed to practice sitting. The monk overseeing our training instructed me to "penetrate into emptiness." I continued to repeat the mantra "*mu, mu . . .*" ("no, no . . ."). The fact that I had a sincere desire to settle my troubled ego was likely why I was able to strive so diligently to honestly penetrate nothingness. After that week, when I was returning home on the Yokosuka train, simply sitting there, outside the landscape seemed so beautiful; inside I was naturally overflowing with a feeling of happiness. Even now, that experience vividly rushes back to me. Dispensing with reason, that practice taught me how I should live, how I could make intelligent use of this life.

Because of my personal experience, I hold the deep conviction that the act of becoming one with emptiness, with no-self, even if for only a short span of time, has the power to radically transform one's life. I maintained my practice of meditation after that experience, and also took up training in the martial art called *kajima shinryu*. Now I spend each day with a feeling of wonder and gratitude for being alive.

I won't suggest that meditation and fencing are for everyone. But I will say that we must, when we are young, commit ourselves to mastering some sort of discipline by losing ourselves in it, by becoming one with it. If we push ourselves in this way, that "self" that lives only for self-satisfaction and is inclined to ego-attachment, will slowly recede, to be replaced by a well-rounded self, capable of discerning true goodness and virtue, and ready to weather the storms of life.

13

FINDING HEALTH
DEEP WITHIN THE MIND

AS A GRADUATE STUDENT, I initially pursued training in the department of maritime products, a part of the Faculty of Agriculture. My research involved tracing habutoglobin—a type of hemoglobin found in human beings—in fish. I ended up finding the same habutoglobin that human beings produce occurs also in twenty different varieties of fish. This was really an exciting discovery for me, and it led me to the much larger conceptual understanding that all life is one. Pondering this concept, I ended up much more interested in contemplating life itself than in looking at fish blood.

Using the objective, analytical means of science to study the nature of life itself is like studying the image in a mirror. What I really wanted to do was to study the mirror itself, this lived experience of being alive, rather than whatever is reflected in it. As a result, I dropped my research on fish and took up Indian Buddhist philosophy instead. Around the same time I began to practice Zen meditation.

It is, of course, important to know about the genes and DNA, without which life would be impossible. But it is also important to know about the "self," the questioning mind that looks into these genes and DNA for answers about life. A reductionist approach to understanding life ends with genes and DNA. This amount of knowledge certainly brings forth amazing results and should be pursued. However, reducing life to its fundamental building blocks will not tell us how to find meaning in it, or how to live it well.

Recently Dr. Richard Dawkins' book *The Selfish Gene* has become a popular topic of discussion. In this book Dr. Dawkins explains that mothers protect their children even at the cost of their own lives, not out of love for the child, but because the genetic imperative is to perpetuate the genetic line. Here a contrast is made between the love of the mother on one hand and the plan or strategy of the genes on the other. The former is rejected and the latter is affirmed. This is a vision of life obtained by focusing on understanding life at the level of DNA and genes.

The question is, is this a sufficient vision of life? Who can decide that birds have no motherly love? When applied to human beings, this view will lead to the conclusion that a human being is nothing more than a vehicle for selfish genes and DNA. What then of human love or compassion toward others? Grasping all of these as nothing other than the strategies of selfish genes is a very dry and tasteless view of life. Life is much fuller, more complex than this.

The chain of cause and effect is not only relevant to the causality of *things*. It is equally relevant to the causality of the mind. Strictly speaking, it may not even be correct to think of these two parts of reality as being distinct from one another. Are mind and matter really the two halves of reality?

Consider the Buddhist understanding of sense organs, such as the eye. Buddhists speak of eyesight as literally "eye-consciousness" and refer to the corresponding sense organ as "the faculty of sight." The visual sense organ, the eye, is an immensely powerful faculty, because it supports vision, the ability to see anything from the biggest galaxy to the smallest particles. The sense organ of the eye consists of a crystalline lens, a cornea, a retina, and so on. In other words it is a "thing," ultimately comprised of atoms and molecules. But how does a thing like the eye produce a mind like vision? Certainly sight occurs, even if it cannot be directly, objectively, non-inferentially shared from individual to individual. So Buddhists limit their understanding of the eye to thinking of it only as "a root of seeing."

The "roots" of sensation are actually twofold. The physical sense organs are called "cooperating roots," whereas the sense data that interact with sense organs are called "actual roots." In the case of vision, its actual root is the field of pure form, color, and shape that interacts with the apparatus of the eye. From the scientific point of view, light waves along the visible portion of the electromagnetic spectrum strike the retina of the eye and are transduced into electrochemical signals that travel down the optic nerves to the brain, where they become sight as we know it.

But from the Buddhist perspective, the actual roots of pure form, color, and shape are projected onto the instantaneously fluctuating field of visible light, rendering them into sensible data. Even the very ideas of form, color, and shape are produced within our own minds, rather than out there in the world. As the seeds laid by various prior actions come to fruition as the people and environments we encounter, so too do the most basic seeds that render the mass of sensory information intelligible come to fruition.

It is same with our other senses and their corresponding sense organs—ear, nose, tongue, and body. According to this thinking, our bodies, endowed with these five sense organs, radiate the energy of sensation from the whole body. Science has yet to devote much attention to the creative role we ourselves play in the world we experience. This way of thinking comes from the conviction that sensation only comes through an experiencer, as we can observe by quietly turning our attention inward toward the mind in yogic meditation.

We have asked whether the mind is in the body or the body is in the mind. But we cannot answer this question. Even if we think, "The mind is X," the mind being thought of in this way can itself never become an object of thought. This leaves us with the problem of understanding what the mind is. For starters, the mind is not a three-dimensional object that possesses size and shape. So, although we speak of it in this way, it doesn't really make sense to say something is "inside" or "outside" of the mind. Some say that the mind is just an epiphenomenon of the brain, like the whirring sound produced by clockwork. This is an interesting idea, but it is not a substantial answer.

Let's move away from this trend of only seeking the cause of things in a material basis. Let's investigate here the relationship between body and mind proposed in Representation Only doctrine, which bases itself on the principle of the oneness of mind and matter. The body is produced by the store consciousness, which is the deepest layer of mind, and there exists a mutual causal relationship between the body and the store consciousness. The relationship between the mind and the body is such that when the mind is disturbed, it will affect the body, and when the body is disturbed, it will affect the mind. We know this from common experience of ulcers following on prolonged periods of stress, or of extreme physical fatigue following deep depression.

This notion of the deep interdependence of body and mind teaches us that if we wish to have good physical health, we must pay attention to the mind. And if we are striving to improve our minds, we must pay attention to the body. To purify the mind at its deepest level, we should proceed first by disciplining the body. When we practice meditation, we begin with the position called the "lotus posture." This posture consists in the mutual arrangement of the left and right legs atop one another, straightening the backbone, pushing the crown of the head slightly upward, and rooting the coccyx into the earth. Indian yogis consider this posture of the body the best position from which to begin meditation.

The state of the body is referred to as comportment. Comportment is used as a technical term in Buddhist monastic texts, where it is synonymous with a dignified bearing. Buddhists list four types of comportment: walking, standing, sitting, and lying down. When we assume these postures with grace and mindfulness we have a dignified bearing. The Buddha trained his monks to care about their comportment at all times as a means of keeping the mind balanced and peaceful. The Zen master Dōgen famously used the phrase, "A dignified bearing is buddhahood" (*igisoku buppo*). What he means to tell us is that truth is not somewhere in a far away place, but it exists right here in our bodies, in the daily affairs of life. These words are meant to make us aware of the importance of the state of the body.

How do we find health deep within the mind? We begin by attending to the superficial states of the body. Devoting ourselves to some discipline, like meditation or fencing, and striving to become one with our training is, counter intuitively, a means of finding health deep within the mind. When we devote ourselves deeply to something, we feel refreshed. We may think of this as merely the alleviation of stress. But from the point of view of Representation Only philosophy, we are actually feeling the results of purifying the mind from the depths of the store consciousness upwards. We are becoming healthy from the depths of our minds upwards.

We all experience a sort of meandering exploration when we are young. The wonder of the Representation Only approach to these issues is that the interdependence of mind and body, of experience and the world experienced, means that we can begin to transform ourselves in simple and easy to handle ways, like devoting a bit of attention to how we carry ourselves, how we sit in the lecture hall, and how we interact with others. It is only when we begin to see that we are active contributors to our life experience, and that there is value in meeting the challenge of taking up a great aim in life, of training ourselves physically and mentally through devotion to meditation or other disciplines, that we begin to really live an intelligent life.

Index

About the Author

Koitsu Yokoyama (b. 1940) devoted his career to the study of Representation Only or Consciousness Only (*vijñaptimātra*) Buddhist philosophy during the second period in the development of Mahāyāna Buddhism. A Buddhist Studies scholar, Yokoyama earned his doctorate in Indian Philosophy at the graduate school of Tokyo University and is currently an Honorary Professor at Rikkyo University and Vice Chancellor of Shogen Junior College. He has published many works in Japanese on Consciousness Only philosophy, including *A Consciousness Only Dictionary of Buddhism,* which was published to commemorate the 1300th anniversary of the Kofukuji Temple in Nara, Japan.

Also Available
from Wisdom Publications

Nothing Is Hidden
The Psychology of Zen Koans
Barry Magid

"A nuanced, sensitive, and compassionate analysis. This book can help point toward more honest introspection that will yield healing and acceptance."—*Publishers Weekly*

The Attention Revolution
Unlocking the Power of the Focused Mind
B. Alan Wallace
Foreword by Daniel Goleman

"Indispensable for anyone wanting to understand the mind. A superb, clear set of exercises that will benefit everyone."—Paul Ekman, Professor Emeritus at University of California San Francisco and author of *Telling Lies* and *Emotions Revealed*

Living Yogacara
An Introduction to Consciousness-Only Buddhism
Tagawa Shun'ei
Translated and introduced by Charles Muller

"This book, expertly translated by Charles Muller, is exceptional for making an extremely complex tradition accessible to the general reader."—*Buddhadharma*

BUDDHIST PSYCHOLOGY
The Foundation of Buddhist Thought, Volume 3
Geshe Tashi Tsering
Edited by Gordon McDougall
Foreword by Lama Zopa Rinpoche

"A user's manual for the human psyche!"—Lorne Ladner, author of *The Lost Art of Compassion*

WHO IS MY SELF?
A Guide to Buddhist Meditation
Ayya Khema

"A truly astonishing book. Ayya Khema is a meditator's meditator, a real expert, as clear about the nuts and bolts of technique as she is about the basic sanity and profound peacefulness that is the goal of all technique."—Norman Fischer, co-abbot, San Francisco Zen Center